SHADOWS *of* CHICAGO

The True Story of Three Men and the Crimes That Shocked America

Shadows of Chicago

The True Story of Three Men and the Crimes that Shocked America

By

Matthew Drew

Shadows of Chicago: The True Story of Three Men and the Crimes That Shocked America

Copyright © 2013 by Matthew Drew
Front cover illustration Copyright © 2013 Matt Cosgrove
Interior Design by Michael Kleen

First Edition published by Black Oak Media, Inc. in 2013

All rights reserved. No part of this book may be reproduced or transmitted in any form or by any means including photocopying, recording, or by any information storage and retrieval system, without written permission from the copyright owner, except for the inclusion of brief quotations in an article or review.

First Printing Summer 2013

ISBN-13: 978-1-61876-018-0

Published by Black Oak Media, Inc.

To order copies of this book contact:

Black Oak Media, Inc.
Rockford, Illinois
www.blackoakmedia.org
orders@blackoakmedia.org

Printed in the United States of America.

To my supportive family and friends.

Contents

THE GREAT FIRE 9
FROM THE ASHES 19
COMMY 25
BIG JIM 43
FREDDY 51
THE CURSED FIRST WARD 57
THE HITLESS WONDERS 67
BIG JIM'S FIGHT 79
HIGH PRESSURE ON BUSSE 91
FRIDAY AT COMISKEY PARK 99
THE WATCHDOGS AND THE YARDS 103
THE THANKSGIVING WARNING 119
THE GREAT STOCKYARD FIRE 127
BIG JIM'S SPIRIT FIGHTS ON 147
END FOR BUSSE AND THE LEVEE 155
THE BLACK SOX 171
EPILOGUE 191
WORKS CITED 205

Chapter 1

THE GREAT FIRE

Baseball was the wildest sport in America. Young ball players played untamed from one side of the country to the other. That was until more and more organized leagues began to assemble.

In 1871, the nation's focus was on the hottest organized team, the unbeatable Cincinnati Red Stockings and their ongoing rampage from coast-to-coast. To the surprise of everyone, a relatively unknown team (also from the Midwest) threatened to end their first-place streak.

The Chicago White Stockings, in their first true year in organized baseball, surprised everyone with a win against the champs, even finishing third in the league. The Red Stockings won the league championship again, but many sports writers predicted Chicago would take it the following year. No one could have predicted that the following season a natural catastrophe would keep the White Stockings from winning a league championship for years to come.

On the Southwest Side of Chicago, children adored their White Stockings, even though most never had a hot ticket to a game. Regardless if they saw a game or not, they dressed like their favorite players by wearing white flannel caps, shirts, stockings, and blue trousers. They also mirrored their favorite players' style to outwit their peers, like the cheating-over technique to force players to hit to their weak side, sacrifice hitting, tag-dodging slides, or plank-style diving catches. Some of the more aggressive techniques sacrificed the body so much they'd end up as road kills.

As children sought to perfect the skills of their favorite players, they were also inventing new ways of winning. One unique method was trash-talking the other team members—an insult directed at one's family member could throw off the best player's game. Besides the trickery, children were adapting to faster and faster play that relied on quicker and quicker thinking. Much of the speedy, imaginative play developing on the wild prairies on the Southwest Side of Chicago would have a direct influence on the future of the professional baseball league.

Many of baseball's most influential pioneers began playing a field nicknamed the "Sandlot," located just southwest of the city. The Sandlot resembled nothing like diamonds children play on today; instead, it looked more like a trampled dirt prairie, speckled with wild grass. The rough ground caused balls to jet in every direction, causing a menace to those fielding them. The ricocheting balls must have been even more difficult to retrieve with their bare hands, and if the kids were lucky to have gloves, they were worn, tattered, sometimes hand-me-downs from older brothers—the rest of the equipment was just as improvised.

It must have been especially challenging to play at the Sandlot on October 8, 1871. On the unusually hot, sunny day, the field's rugged ground must have been worse as ever, since most of the grass had been depleted from weeks of baking, arid weather. But that day, for young Charles Comiskey, Fred Busse and Jim Horan, the challenging conditions made the game more exciting.

At only twelve-years-old, Jim Horan and Charles Comiskey amazed others with their aggressive play, crushing the ball and snagging anything hit their way. Meanwhile, Fred Busse, a few years younger, played unnoticeably in the background, secretly admiring his friends' aggressiveness on the field. Young Fred Busse was particularly thrilled to watch Jim Horan's play—his mom and Jim Horan's mom were close friends and he looked up to him for as long as he could remember.

Matthew Drew

The Sandlot was the boys' innocent escape from the weekly brawls between ethnic groups surrounding their neighborhood. It was common for them to see gangs of boys armed with butcher knives, rusty hooks, awls, and various farm tools looking for a fight. The hottest rivalry was between ethnic immigrants and the "Nativists," a ragtag group of rowdy, mostly Protestant, ethnic Anglo-Saxons who shared a common hatred for "anti-American" cultures and banded together to fight off "enemies" encroaching on their prairie land, mostly being the Irish and Germans.

Nativists, both young and old, along with many other white-Anglos, believed the Irish were a dangerous, worthless race of mongrels. Much of this hatred had existed through centuries of conflicts in Europe between the Irish and English. More recent prejudices in the States existed because the Irish immigrants were seen as stupid peasant farmers who spent all their time drinking, fighting, and committing violent crimes. Although many Irish were proven troublemakers, many didn't realize they provided an enormous hand in building the nation. For instance, the Irish recently fought heroically on both sides of the Civil War and worked tenaciously building roads and waterways—most notably, the Illinois and Michigan Canal.[1] Nevertheless, the Irish in Chicago would spend the next half a century shrugging off racist attacks—many storefront signs would read "No Irish Need Apply"—and seemingly endless racial slurs such as "Turkey" and "Paddy" would resound throughout the streets. As a result of the prejudices, the Chicago Irish found kinship in parish-centered neighborhoods with their own kind.

Crime was not the only thing fueling many of the Nativists' hatred towards newly-arrived ethnic groups. Much of the hatred stemmed from the drunken behavior of Irish and Germans in public. To stop their seemingly bizarre drinking routine, mobs of Nativists, along with a band of conservative Christian groups, spearheaded heated protests throughout the city. Once the mobs found their rants and raves were met with jokes and laughs, they called on their main supporter, the mayor of Chicago, Roswell Mason, to enact anti-liquor laws on Sundays—already the mayor had their support because he sought to end the amount of saloons during his administration. So, with the help of the mayor, they were able to "slow down" the amount of drinking on Sundays. This especially infuriated the Germans who spent every Sunday at beer gardens, some of the liveliest places in the city. The neighborhood "biergartens" imitated the ones they remembered from southern Germany: most had open air areas with trees, wooden benches, and gravel ground, and day and night you could hear loud laughing, blaring folk music, and the smell of pipes and cigars permeated the air.

German and Irish alike saw no problem with their festive drinking habits, as long as it didn't interfere with work the next day. They were able to find jobs, despite many efforts of Nativists and other xenophobic Chicagoans to keep them out of their workforce. The Irish typically found jobs as laborers, while many Germans became butchers in the stockyards or small business owners. Although Irish and Germans had similar struggles, they typically banded with their own kind in separate neighborhoods. This was true with Jim Horan's and Charles Comiskey's Irish families, and Fred Busse's German family. They started off away from where they were not wanted.

Even though the three friends were born in the U.S. like other Nativists, they still always had to watch their backs walking to their homes near the block of 100 West 18th Street, several blocks south of the Sandlot.

Despite the inherent dangers of walking the streets, that hot, sunny afternoon must have seemed normal. On the other hand, nothing seemed normal to the U.S. Weather Service in Chicago as they tracked the unusually dry conditions for that time of year. Only 5.27 inches of rain fell in the city from July to October, instead of the average 9-

Matthew Drew

plus inches that normally fell during that time period. So unusual were these conditions that the dry weather caused the leaves to drop as early as July.[2]

Their walk home that day took them along the sidewalks, a series of rotting wood planks haphazardly placed along the sides of the road. These planks were designed to protect citizens from getting stuck in the mud or trampled by horses or buggies. They were so prevalent they connected most of the wood houses and storefronts throughout Chicago. All in all, the entire city was like an archaic town, consisting of buildings slapped together with little or no regard for fire-resistant materials or construction methods. In addition, stored between many of these buildings were bundles of firewood, the same type residents used to burn in fireplaces, as well as coal for furnaces. As a result, just about all of the buildings sat like powder kegs waiting for even the most minor spark that could trigger a major city-wide inferno. Strangely, this ominous warning was revealed to readers in the morning *Tribune*.

After the boys returned home that day, each of them probably went to sleep early to go to school in the morning. Shortly after falling asleep at about 9:00 p.m., a fire broke out in the O'Leary barn a few blocks away, causing them to awake to the sounds of screaming men, women, and children. To their horror they soon would discover their neighbors wearing torn, filthy pajamas, their bodies covered in soot, quickly moving from the fire burning behind them. The peculiar scene was illuminated by the enormous fire only a couple of blocks away.

The same streets the boys may have walked earlier that afternoon were now engulfed by a red-orange fire spiraling a hundred feet into the sky. The clear, star-filled night was draped by a dense-black smoke cloud speckled with glowing embers. The fire below reflected off the dark smoke cloud, making the scene even more astonishing to their young eyes. They must have felt hopeless as they stared at the terrible beauty of the rising inferno.

They were awestruck as the fire sprawled quickly throughout the city. It traveled from building to building along the dry wood sidewalks, racing in the direction of the oxygen-rich east wind originating from the Iowa plains. As the 30mph wind pushed the fire north, masses of superheated air rose from the flames, causing a whirling motion upon contact with the cooler surrounding air from Lake Michigan. One observer who witnessed the whirling fire said, "The fire came from the air above, more than [what burned] from the earth." The fire winds funneling from the sky scorched buildings in seconds. The newly created fires spread through entire neighborhoods in minutes, creating a sickening stench of burnt timber, and animal and human flesh. Most of the sounds were the roar of the fire and the screaming people escaping the flames.[3]

As some survivors scurried away from the flames, firefighters remained to fight back the spreading inferno. Their attempts to drench the encroaching hundred-foot fire walls with hoses were futile because the hoses didn't provide the necessary amount of water needed to make an effective offensive stance. This was due to the hundreds of feet of hose charged at the same time, requiring too much water pressure from the horse-drawn engines and hydrants—because fire engineering laws rule that water pressure is adversely affected the longer the length of hose. Even if the firefighters had used shorter lengths in this case, most of the small engines weren't powerful enough to draw the enormous amount of water necessary from the hydrants. Moreover, the water mains were not large enough to sustain the streams necessary soak such a gigantic fire.

The three-and-a-half square-mile fire proved to be too much for the sixteen horse-drawn steam engines (although the most modern of the day) of the Chicago Fire Department. On top of that, there were only six hose carts, four hook and ladder companies, and 185 firemen—a little more than half of those working this particular day. The few working firefighters were on a first-shift system, 24 hour breaks between shifts.[4] To add to the difficulties, some firemen worked multiple shifts that kept them awake for several days in a row and most had fought a fire that almost burnt down the city the night before.[5]

There were 28 major fires during the week, making the situation so dire that the First Fire Marshal Robert A. Williams had spent the past several days pressing city government for emergency measures. His appeal to city council for greater resources, particularly John Comiskey (Charles's father), fell on deaf ears just as it had in the past. For the last year with the help of the Board of Police and Fire Commissioners, Marshal Williams lobbied unsuccessfully for more fire hydrants, floating steam engines on the Chicago River, a limitation of wood as a building material, and larger water mains. Additionally, he requested 15,000 feet of new hose, but he received only 10,000 feet. More importantly, he said the fire department was spread too thin, incapable of protecting its 36 square miles. Regardless of what would have happened if his requests were granted, or if political maneuvering were to blame for the fire, it's important to recognize the red tape involved when fighting for the city's safety.[6]

Even though the fire department and politicians knew there was a drastic need to improve safety measures, this day firefighters were not equipped to contain such a massive blaze. As a result, they were forced to defend areas by using a method similar to a "controlled burn" used in wilderness firefighting. The tactic used in this case was to remove fuel from the path of the fire so it burned itself out. This process was initiated with the help of Civil War hero General Philip Sheridan along with other Union soldier vets, who purposely ignited and exploded whole blocks of buildings in an attempt to plug the fire's path of destruction.[7] In other areas they purposely directed the fire east toward Lake Michigan by stacking fuel along a trail until the fire drowned in the water. All along the lakefront the fires followed the "controlled" trails until they sizzled, steamed, and expired in the cool water.

Despite best efforts to control the fire, it raged for two days and nights. The agonizing fight ended on the morning of October 10th after light rains doused what remained of the flames. After the last flame was extinguished, 15,700 buildings were destroyed from Harrison Street north to Fullerton Avenue, and from the Chicago River east to Lake Michigan. The only buildings not ruined were on the outskirts of town, including the Union Stockyards. As a result of the devastation, 100,000 men, women and children were left homeless and up to 300 people perished.[8]

"Ruins of Chicago." View of Clark Street looking north after the Chicago Fire of 1871; Chicago Fire; 1871; Lithographer-- Gregson. Chicago History Museum, #i02968

Matthew Drew

For days after the fire, the three boys watched hundreds of homeless refugees lugging their few valuables past their homes, away from the still-smoking destruction. Their families and they had escaped homelessness and possibly death only because the wind blew north instead of south. It was a humbling experience to know they were at the mercy of such a powerful unforeseen force. At the same time, it was such a horrific experience as to haunt them the rest of their days—no one more than Jim Horan.

---

[1] The Illinois Michigan canal was built mostly by Irish immigrants. Many died during its construction. The project connected the Chicago River with the Mississippi, increasing trade throughout the Midwest.

[2] "The Weather Doctor Almanac 2000," www.islandnet.com

[3] Sawislak, Karen. *Smoldering City: Chicago and the Great Fire, 1871-1874*. Chicago: University of Chicago Press, 1995.

[4] Bales, Richard F. *The Great Chicago Fire and the Myth of Mrs. O'Leary's Cow*. McFarland Press.

[5] Sawislak.

[6] Sawislak & Bales.

[7] General Sheridan, who lived in Chicago since 1867, was assigned all police authority during and sometime after The Great Fire by the ineffectual Mayor Rowell Mason. Many people, including Civil War veterans questioned this decision, having witnessed some Sheridan's brutality, including his massacre of Southerners and the Cheyenne Tribe.

[8] Bales.

Shadows of Chicago

Chapter 2

FROM THE ASHES

At midnight the first night of the Great Chicago Fire, Conley's Patch, the Irish south side ghetto that ran from 12th to 16th streets and from Michigan Avenue to the Lake, burnt entirely to the ground. The wretched quarter had been full of hundreds of poorly built shanties and the largest haven for slum of and vice in the city. During Chicago's short history before the fire, Irish hoodlums from the area would terrorize people in all sections of city and then, most often times, scurry safely back to their neighborhood.

Conley's Patch, which had for so long been their refuge, was gone, scattering criminals from the ghetto to different areas of the city. In spite of this change, the hoodlums' shenanigans would continue and, as they got older, their crimes would graduate from burglary and pickpocketing to seedier, politically-backed crimes, with many becoming top members of Chicago's underworld.

The most notorious Irish rogues to come from Conley's Patch were "Bathhouse" John Coughlin and Michael "Hinky-Dink" Kenna. About the same age as Busse, Horan, and Comiskey, they were already aggressively on the make. Kenna, who lived in a frame shack at the edge of the neighborhood, left school at the age of 12 and purchased a newsstand at Monroe and Dearborn streets. On the side, he did odd jobs for saloon keepers, developing friendships with prostitutes and other outcasts.

John Coughlin, equally entrepreneurial, worked at his father's grocery store (that he eventually lost to the Great Fire). At first he followed his father's respectable living and went to school. Soon though, he got a job at a Turkish bathhouse (hence the nickname "Bathhouse") on

Shadows of Chicago

Clark Street, where he rubbed elbows with the most powerful, sometimes most rotten people in the city. Coughlin said later in life, "I watched and learned [at the bathhouses] never to quarrel, never to feud. I had the best schooling a young feller could have." Needless to say, even at such a young age, both hoodlums found that real power and money were in politics—and now that the city was in ruins, it was the best time for crime to flourish.

Less criminal-minded survivors like the Comiskey, Horan, and Busse families set their sights on future progress and rebuilding the city. However, progress was slowed by a few who felt the need to blame someone or something. A few wasted their time blaming the O'Leary family along with a number of other innocent people. There were others who professed that the fire was a result of God punishing the city for its brazen immorality.[1]

To convince others of the reason for God's sudden wrath, religious groups alluded to the brothels on Wells Street and to the liquor, gambling, prostitution, and crime. Although most knew these vices had been part of Chicago's dichotomy since the frontier days, a growing number of people believed that the fire's aftermath was as good an opportunity as ever to abolish vice from the city forever. Subsequently, a few ordinary citizens banded with religious zealots for a war against immorality in the city, setting the stage for a conflict that would affect the entire nation for decades to come. This war against wickedness would mostly prove to be a losing battle right after the fire, because just about every politician wanted to build a new city reflective of their personal interests—some of those included white-slavery, illegal booze, gambling, shady business dealings, and vote-buying. Politicians knew that there were rich opportunities in indulgences, especially during difficult times, so they would either engage in the corruption or turn a blind eye to it.

Matthew Drew

Two years prior to the fire, citizens attempted to rid the city of filth by voting for Mayor Roswell Mason on the People's Party ticket (soon to be known as the Democratic Party). Mason was seen as a hard-working, accomplished engineer with high moral standards. Evidently, for the most part, he was morally sound, especially compared to other politicians who followed him. However, contrary to his reputation, he did little to end the city of corruption, either because he didn't care enough or maybe because the job was too demanding.[2] One reporter in *The Chicago Times* described him "a self-avowed lame duck" who desired to leave public office. The *Times* added: "One mason who will never help rebuild the city—Mayor Mason." Even though *The Times* had usually smeared his name, his few remaining People's Party supporters abandoned him as well after he did little to help rebuild the city after the fire.

Coincidentally, the fire hit the city less than a month before it was time to elect a new mayor, in turn, causing a new, distorted political firestorm. Then, more than ever before, there was two-party mudslinging, similar to elections we have today. The battle between the People's Party and Republican Party in Chicago was heating up just as it had on the East Coast, for meanwhile, in newspapers across the country, headlines declared that the Boss Tweed ring had fallen, causing local Republicans to state that the shameful Democratic voter fraud that was going on in New York, was also happening in Chicago.[3] Furthermore, Republicans pointed to examples of favoritism and nepotism that existed in Democratic city politics. To act upon these sentiments, Republican Party members developed a group known as the Union Fireproofers—the name was a bold attempt to exploit the aftermath of the fire for political benefit. The Fireproofers were mostly a group of wealthy local businessmen whose foremost claim was that honesty in city politics can be best achieved by using their talents they learned in the big business world.

Shadows of Chicago

So, who best to represent their interests but nationally recognized Republican and *Chicago Tribune* owner Joseph Medill? His stiff, big-business demeanor contrasted with the demonstrative mayoral candidates before him—the latter opting for a less formal political manner. It was not surprising that *Trib* writers overwhelmingly favored their boss, because he controlled their livelihood. It was surprising, however, that most *Chicago Times* writers, who had traditionally supported the Democratic Party and had bashed past Republican candidates, now were supporting Medill. Democrats agreed with Republicans that Medill's uncontroversial manner would improve the city's image. So, it was neither his political experience nor his oral expertise that made him such a preferred candidate, but it was mostly due to people's distaste with Chicago politicians. The time was right for Medill to bump right into the mayor's position, just as Fred Busse would decades later.[4]

During Medill's first year in office, he was viewed by many as a heroic figure at the forefront of helping to rebound the city from devastation. On the surface there could be no denying it, for workers from around the country poured into the city like never before, building new buildings constructed with brick and mortar. The construction market was rich with opportunity.

Construction seemed to be the biggest industry, but in actuality, the "pleasure" industry was becoming richest market. The First Ward's red-light district became the largest in the U.S. During the first eight months after the Chicago Fire, the city granted 2,218 saloon licenses—that's one for every 150 citizens. Liquor poured into the city at a rate never seen before, as well as drugs. Drugs users, who always hid in back alleys, were now shooting-up in the open. Also, prostitutes, who had usually kept out of the public eye, were now seen standing stark-naked in doorways, hollering to citizens passing by.[5]

Soon though, the majority of prostitutes started conducting their business from 18th to 22nd streets, between Wabash and Clark, the area commonly called The Levee. The Levee's new open sex market would introduce the most entrepreneurial madams throughout the country. The most brazen of all, the Everleigh sisters, Ada and Minna, would come to Chicago decades later.

At about the time of The Great Chicago Fire, Ada and Minna Simms (Everleigh) were being raised in an aristocratic atmosphere in Virginia. Their parents would be appalled that his daughters would one day open the greatest brothel in the country and become the most infamous madams in the nation's history.[6]

---

[1] The Great Chicago Fire originated near the O'Leary home on DeKoven Street on the Near Southwest Side of the city, only a few blocks from the Horan, Comiskey and Busse homes. The O'Leary family was often hounded by people looking to place blame for the fire, particularly Catherine O'Leary and her cow that allegedly kicked over the lantern. Another hypothesis suggests that simultaneous fire outbreaks occurring in Chicago, Peshtigo, Wisconsin and Manistee, Michigan were sparked by remnants of the Comet Biela. The Peshtigo fire started at the same minute as the one in Chicago, wiping out the entire town in a few hours. 1,182 people died and 1.25 acres were destroyed as a result of the fire, almost 4 times the damage of The Great Chicago Fire.

[2] Mark, Norman. *Mayors Madams & Madmen*. Chicago: Chicago Review Press, 1979.

[3] William "Boss" Tweed was a politician from the House of Representatives and then the Senate who ran the Democratic machine out of New York's Tammany Hall. Throughout the 19th Century he controlled political patronage in New York City and the New York State. He was found guilty of corruption and died in jail.

[4] Mark.

[5] Abbott, Karen. *Sin in the Second City. Madams, Ministers, Playboys and the Battle for America's Soul*. New York: Random House, 2007.

[6] Abbott.

Shadows of Chicago

Chapter 3
COMMY

Charles Comiskey's father, John, moved from Ireland during the Potato Famine. The only thing he had with him when he arrived in Chicago was a hard-nosed work ethic and a thirst for making it big. His determination quickly moved him from a laborer up to a brick construction contractor. His knack for business was so appealing he was voted political boss of his Chicago ward, served as alderman, and then became president of the city council. From the second he arrived at City Hall, people saw him as breath of fresh air from the flashy politicians that spewed out whatever the people wanted to hear. John's straightforward, speak-not-just-to-be-heard approach was popular. His noble manner was so appealing everyone throughout the city knew him as "Honest John."[1]

Despite his popularity within the political realm, he was seen as a frugal menace to the fire department. As a matter of fact, it was he who denied First Fire Marshal Williams' dire requests for crucial safety measures. If the marshal's requests were heeded, the fire's devastation would not have been as extensive. Then again, John could not have fathomed that such a cataclysmic event could have happened, even if he knew his brick business would benefit from a major conflagration. Either way, the fire's aftermath allowed him to capitalize on city brick building contracts, making him one of wealthiest people in the city. And not surprisingly, one of his first contracts was to rebuild City Hall.[2]

John wanted to instill his tough-as-nails business sense into his children. He hated idleness and play, insisting that work and education were the way to succeed.

Shadows of Chicago

He was especially tough on his son Charles, the third of his eight children. Charles Comiskey was born to John and Annie (nee Kearns) in Chicago on August 15, 1859. Since he was a child, John dreamt that Charles would become a successful businessman and did anything to keep his son away from wasting his time playing baseball (which he called a "frivolous game"), even sending him to school in Wisconsin during the school year. Conversely, his mother, with whom he was close, accepted his dreams to play baseball for a living.[3]

As a child, Charles hid his dreams from his father, acting like any other youngster, helping around the house, but then, when his father went to work, spent every free moment playing ball at the Sandlot. It wouldn't be until years later that he gathered enough nerve to show his father his life's passion.

* * * *

On a hot summer's day in 1876, 17-year-old Charles Comiskey sat in the driver's seat, holding the reins of his father's brick wagon as it rolled along the cobblestoned street. He and his fellow workers used the time to get a breather before the next job. This hot summer's day in 1876 had been as busy as ever and there were few jobs that were hotter than brick business, both literally and figuratively: much of the city still lay in ruins, opening the market for brick and mortar. Few customers wanted wood construction, fearing another disaster—the Great Chicago Fire was a learning experience for all.[4]

Charles and the rest of the crew were two miles away from their next big drop off; when at the corner of Jackson and Laflin streets he suddenly stopped the horses and heavy load. From his position in the driver's seat he now had a

Matthew Drew

bird's-eye view of rivalry between two of the best local baseball teams, the Liberties and the Franklins. Charles, an avid Liberties fan, noticed its pitcher struggling on the mound, for there was little relief pitching in those days—match-ups could last until it was too dark to play anymore. Frustrated by pounding the pitcher took, and foreseeing a certain romp by the Franklins, he dropped the reins, hopped down from the brick wagon, strolled over, and grabbed the ball from the team's pitcher.

It must have been surprising for all to watch this six-foot, lanky kid dressed in work clothes now in charge of stopping the Franklins from certain domination. Equally surprising, Charles struck out the side with a series of fastballs, stinging the catcher's hands—every catcher complained of his burning fastballs.

Meanwhile, two miles to the northeast, customers hollered because they had not received their brick shipment. Charles's father, John, could not contact his son by telephone (it had just been invented in early March of that year), so after some time, he made the painful discovery in person. To his horror, he found his son playing on the field, while a load of bricks and crew sat idle next to the ball park. His Irish temper fumed, but instead of dragging his son off the ball field by his ear, John retrained himself, jumped atop the wagon's bay, and called for the driver to depart.

Meanwhile, Charles finished the game, probably with some apprehension about abandoning his father. It's unknown if the Liberties won or how his father reacted when he got home, but later in life he revealed that this was the moment he found his calling in life.[5]

Charles admitted that his "walk-on" success that summer day gave him the momentum to pursue his baseball career. The following season, he played ball for St. Mary's College in Kansas. Right away, his wild play, some said as wild as the Chicago prairies where he first learned the game, quickly set him apart from other players on the team. It took only a few games for players and fans to notice his amazing ability to make a defensive play just about anywhere in the field, even if balls were nowhere near his position. They were equally amazed at his offensive game, especially his ability stretch a single or get on base no matter what. Right away his teammates called him "Commy," a nickname probably derived from his last name, but it may have also been because he had commanded his teammates like a *comm*issioner.

No one noticed his quick-thinking, enthusiastic play more than Timothy "Ted" Sullivan. Ted was a few years older, a pitcher-manager for the team, and had an insatiable eye for talent—a gift that would one day make him the one of the most noted organizers in professional baseball. Using his prowess, Ted chose the freshman Commy to be the team's captain. Years later, Ted he explained why: "I picked Comiskey [as captain] because I considered him the smartest kid on the team. One incident will show how quickly, even in those days, he grasped at an opportunity. I noticed that a runner on third was taking a rather big lead. Comiskey [as catcher] signaled for a certain ball. I shook my head. He signaled for another and I repeated. Finally I left the box, all the time upbraiding him because of his bonehead strategy. He never said a word but met me half way, and still bawling him out I slipped him the ball while I returned to the mound. All set behind the bat and Comiskey whipped the ball to third nailing the runner by ten feet. I did not tell him what to do. I simply wanted to find out if he could think for himself. From that time on I began to have respect for Charles, and he was only a kid at that."[6]

Even though Commy was wild and uncoachable, Ted became his mentor and improved his play. As a result, Commy and Ted became an inseparable and they both agreed that they could work together to build the best team the sport had to offer.

But the two would have to take a short hiatus from one another when Commy was removed from St. Mary's College after one year and sent to an extremely strict Christian Brothers College in Prairie du Chien, Wisconsin. Instead of buckling down to his studies (as his father would have hoped), he rejoined Ted the following summer in Milwaukee playing for a team called the Alerts. This wasn't bad for a kid still in his teens, and, at 50 dollars a month, it would be his first paid gig. Still, though, the money would not keep him in Milwaukee very long. Once he found out the team's catcher whined to the coach that he threw the ball too hard, the fired-up Commy packed his bags and moved to Elgin, Illinois, to play for the Elgin Watch Team, mostly because he found a catcher who could take the heat he threw. From his teammates' perspectives, they were happy to have him, because he led them to an undefeated season. Despite the publicity he received as result the dominance over the league's teams, he felt he had to go back with Ted if he wanted to one day go to the big leagues.[7]

In 1878, Commy went to Iowa to play ball for a team Ted hoped would propel them towards establishing a professional baseball league. As a favor to his friend, Commy reluctantly took a pay cut during the season, and to make up for his lost wages in the off-season he sold newspapers and magazines for the Illinois Central Railroad. In Iowa, he was a successful pitcher and led the team to a championship in the Northwestern league—this was one of the first minor leagues—many in the league became famous professional ballplayers.

Even though Ted put the league together, neither Ted nor Commy were content in the minors because they wanted to generate more fans and bask in the glory of the big leagues, and, if lucky, get the big bucks.

Since the league did not generate the revenue he had hoped, Ted dropped the league and kept a team called the

Shadows of Chicago

Dubuque Rabbits, a hodgepodge of players from the Northwestern league and few stragglers they found along the road, becoming a successful traveling minor league team. So successful, in fact, they were invited to play an exhibition game against the St. Louis Browns, a professional team at the top of the game.

Not surprising to anyone, the big league Browns slaughtered the minor league Rabbits without allowing any runs. The Rabbits players would go unnoticed, except for Commy, who had an errorless game at first base (luckily he had a worn pitching arm), and had one of the team's two hits, a two-bagger.[8]

With only seeing one game, the Browns organization was so impressed with the young aggressive first basemen they wrote a letter, inviting him to play for up to $125 a month. The time was right for Commy to accept the offer, because he just got married to his favorite girl, Nan Kelly of Dubuque, Iowa.[9] Still, he was reluctant to leave for the big leagues without his buddy Ted, so he felt it best that he ask permission. Once he asked him if it was okay, Ted replied that he was "too good for him anyways." He was probably half-joking.[10]

In 1882, he started his professional career with the St. Louis Browns, but like always, Commy's transition forward would not go smoothly. The fired up, young Commy got into it right away with the equally bombastic owner, Chris Von der Ahe. As soon as he showed up at St. Louis to be a Brown, Von der Ahe expected him to accept his new position at right field. To the owner's surprise, Commy fired back, saying he'd go back to minors if he didn't get the first base position, and, on top of that, he wanted more money. Von der Ahe was so impressed with the young star's bold comeback he handed him the starting first basemen's position, made him captain, and also raised his salary.

He knew right away that fans would be drawn to hoopla around the new prospect, knowing everything about generating revenue but nothing about baseball—one time he even boasted that the Browns had the biggest infield diamond in the world, when everyone else knew that all diamonds are the same size. Van der Ahe didn't even pretend to be interested in the games, so instead of sitting in the stands critiquing the game with higher management, he spent his time in the stadium beer garden laughing wildly, carrying handfuls of beer steins to customers. But with his highs came his lows, one of which came when Van der Ahe fined his star player Bill Gleason for missing a ground ball. The problem was that the ball was so far away from Gleason that a fan had a better chance of grabbing it.[11]

For the most part, Von der Ahe was all smiles when he saw what a hit Commy was with the St. Louis fans. Fans roared and like never before, a record number of beer barrels emptied, profits hit an all-time high all because they wanted to watch the most unique first basemen to ever play the game.

His play seemed so unusual to fans because at the time, first basemen planted themselves near the first base bag waiting for that hard ball thrown at them from third, short, or second. Contrary to other first basemen, Commy would grab a ball deep into right field or just about anywhere, he would always cheat over to second, and hollered and trash-talked the other team. His defensive play was so aggressive that batters on opposite teams would hold back from hitting it to his side, causing hard-pulling lefties or cheating-righties to think twice. G.W. Axelson, the author of Comiskey's biography *Commy,* wrote, "Many a wiseacre who saw Commy playing out on [right field's] grass declared his whole performance 'unnatural,' and they predicted chaos as soon as a hot grounder came out Commy's way. A hot grounder did come his way towards first base, Commy gobbled it up way past the base. To everyone's surprise he threw the ball, almost blindly at first

Shadows of Chicago

to the pitcher who covered the plate and caught the ball and tagged first for an out. To the howl of the fans' delight."[12]

Photograph of Charles A. Comiskey as a ballplayer for the St. Louis Browns, circa 1886.; (n.p.); 1916; Photographer--Chicago Daily News, Inc. Chicago History Museum, #SDN-060606.

Matthew Drew

Fans were equally impressed with his offensive play, but it wasn't for his hitting; he batted a meager .250 or .275 average, and only once above a .300. It was once he was on base that he was a force to be reckoned. He was fast, stealing 62 bases in 1887 and 77 the next year. His quick base running became such a nuisance for opposing pitchers and fielders that they would make costly mistakes trying to get him out. After any minor mistake, he was there to capitalize on getting an extra base. Even if he foresaw getting tagged out, he dove head first and used his signature "hook slide" around the tag. His teammate from the St. Louis Browns, Bill Gleason, described the move best: "The 'hook slide' is simply a physical skill combined with head work... We only varied the performance as the bruises on our body dictated. It was much like broiling a steak. If rare on one side, turn it over. It was before fancy sliding pads had been invented and I want to bear testimony to the fact that the runways were no softer than they are now." Most of the time the maneuver worked well, but one little mistake and you were breaking a nose or jaw, or losing some teeth, but for advantageous players like Commy it was better than the alternative, sliding blindly, legs first—a sure way to be tagged out.

Commy's aggressiveness was contagious. So much so, those players from around the league tried to copy his play, and that is why his teammate Bill Gleason said he was responsible for half the changes teams made throughout the National League.

The Browns' management felt it would be beneficial for the rest of the team to adopt some of Commy's "unnatural" play, so he was made player/manager of the team in 1884. He led the team from first base, constantly yelling to them, telling the shortstop to cover third or second, or telling the outfielders to move way out of position. He had such a commanding presence on the field that players improved their aggressiveness by looking for every opportunity to get into every play, anywhere on the field. More importantly, teammates began backing each other up, letting no balls dribble to the fences. Never had the Browns worked as such a cohesive unit, and under Commy they won four straight pennants and two world championships.

As the years went by, Commy began to spend more time coaching and less time playing the game. He all but disappeared from the batting order and player roster as he got a little older and his stats declined. Most people didn't notice because he was just as active (and amusing) as a coach as he was a player. It was never his way to sit quietly in the dugout; instead, he constantly wiggled and slid along the wooden bench. One time his players tricked him by placing a jagged nail in a hole in the bench along the path of his typical slides. When Commy ran out of the dugout to holler at an umpire's missed call, he revealed to everyone in the stadium his shredded pants near his rear end. Needless to say, he was not as amused as his players were.

Throughout the game he stomped onto the field of play and running down the baseline to holler at his team, opponents, and umpires. Strangely, he wouldn't even be wearing his uniform most of the time. His coaching method was such a menace that the league first introduced the coaching box—these were lines drawn at first and third to be used as barriers for aggressive coaches like Commy—these are still present in fields everywhere. James A. Hart, former president of the Cubs, related to a writer why there are barriers at first and third: "The chalk lines which enclose the coaching boxes were added to the field diagram after Charles Comiskey had demonstrated their necessity," he said. "Comiskey and Gleason used to plant themselves on each side of the visiting catcher and comment on his breeding habits, personal habits, skill as a receiver, or rather lack of it, until the unlucky backstop was unable to tell whether one or a half a dozen balls were coming his way. Not infrequently the umpire came in for a few remarks... This solicitous attention did not add to the efficiency of the backstop, so for the sake of not unduly increasing the population of insane asylums or encouraging justifiable homicide, the coacher's box was invented. This helped out the catcher, but the pitcher and the other players on the opposing team were still at the mercy of Comiskey, and I know of no man who had a sharper tongue, who was in command of more biting sarcasm, or who was quicker at repartee." Every coach and every player in the league knew that if Commy's team wasn't winning he would be preying on every weakness they had. That did not mean he didn't play fair. He did, but he wouldn't accept a loss, much less a losing team.[13]

    He knew that to keep the St. Louis Browns at the top of the National League it was important that he keep the best players out there. Even though he knew his players could easily take a better offer from another team, he felt he could keep most of them as long as he continued to have control of the lineup—this was an unwritten agreement he had with Von der Ahe.

    But the Browns organization slumped when Von der Ahe got a case of tunnel vision and decided he could sell his championship players to make a quick buck, even though he would have continued to make a boat load of money off of Commy's team. He first sold his top stars Mike Kelly and John Clarkson for $20,000 to his rival A.G. Spaulding of the Chicago White Stockings. Soon after, he sold the majority of other star players, including the Commy's favorite player on the team, Bill Gleason—all without his knowledge.

    Commy and the St. Louis fans were infuriated. Instead of joining the rest of the ousted team in a fit of rage, like he would have done before entering the big leagues, Commy decided to stick it out for a raise from $90 a month to $8,000 a year—an impressive amount of money for this

Shadows of Chicago

time period. His decision to stay for more cash perhaps marked the beginning of his abandoning the spirit of the game for a business opportunity.

Not surprising, the St. Louis Browns never again reached the caliber they were at before, and, as an added insult to the organization, they were clobbered by the very players who were sold off—perhaps, in part, because they were onto Commy's wild play tactics.

On an emotional level, this made it especially difficult for Commy to get the team back on track. Even though he was able to recruit some good players, he could never regain the magic he had before Von der Ahe sold off his players. The whole mess became a lesson for him in what owners could do to a ball club.

To insure that the shameful memories in St. Louis wouldn't ruin his credibility as a ball club leader forever, in 1892 Commy took a job as a manager, and occasionally played first base, for the National League's Cincinnati Reds. In Cincinnati, he ran a pretty good team by keeping control of his players, rather than letting them fall into the owners' hands. He went so far as to openly tell the players and the media that NL owners could not be trusted because they were a bunch of deceitful con men.

An unexpected tragic event happened while he travelling by train with his Reds team. In the middle of night, as the team's train was about to arrive in St. Louis, a freight train collided with the team's passenger train, knocking two sleeper cars off the rail couplings, causing the runaway cars to pitch down a slope. As the Reds players exited their car safely, they noticed they were missing their star players Pete Browning and Commy. They were horrified to see the sleeper car where the two slept, sloped down a hill and on fire. The Reds players thought that if they weren't killed by the crash, they'd be certainly killed by the spreading fire.

With the help of the train crew, team members grabbed axes and spikes and began carving a way to reach the trapped men. Once a pathway was created through the mangled steel and scattered debris, they made it to the aisle of the car. It took some effort to get through the green curtains that had fallen from the windows, the bedding, and splinters that covered the aisle. As they pulled away the last obstructions, they expected to find their dead teammates. Instead, Comiskey and Browning were found conscious, dangling comically upside down, and their legs facing towards the ceiling. To the surprise of everyone, neither they nor the other passengers were hurt seriously. Commy just pretended he was mad at the players for waking him up. Even though he joked, the accident must have shaken him up.

He dismissed the accident so he could focus on shaking up the owners of the National League. As he continued to voice his displeasure, Commy's negative opinions caught the ear of Byron Bancroft "Ban" Johnson, a sport's writer for a newspaper in Cincinnati. Ban agreed with Commy's distaste with NL ownership and agreed that something should be done to clean things up. So after months of drinking and card playing together, they devised a plan to uproot the National League's monopoly.

They believed their dream would be a reality if they coerced the best players in the NL to join their new major league division—a difficult task, considering the popularity of the professional league. With this daunting mission in mind, the plan progressed when Commy convinced Ban to run a minor league called the Western League in 1893, centered in the Midwest, while Commy moved back to the minors to run the Sioux City, Iowa, franchise.

Right away, Ban's Western League became very popular among baseball fans. Much of this was due to Ban's shifty marketing techniques. He fluffed-up the Western League by saying it was a clean break from the "dirty game"

Shadows of Chicago

played in the NL and that the new face of baseball would include "everyday" Americans, not just those who could afford hot-ticket games.

As a blatant attempt to attract more of the nation's fans, Ban changed the name from the Western League to the American League in 1900, but he knew it would take a while longer for it to be a big league organization capable of competing with the NL. To do so, he first needed the help of the most powerful league owners and managers, especially Commy. As soon as Commy moved his team from the Sioux City to St. Paul, Ban moved the Grand Rapids franchise to Cleveland (eventually becoming the Cleveland Indians). His ultimate plan was to drop the American League from the National Agreement, a written contract that attempted to keep minor league franchises from organizing into their separate professional leagues and to keep them from gaining NL players. Ban's break from with the agreement eventually would allow teams from Baltimore, Boston, Philadelphia, and Washington, whose players severed ties with the NL because they were angered that owners capped their yearly pay at $2,400—a decent amount of money for the time period, but not as much as many players thought they could be making.

The stage was now set for Commy to turn his St. Paul franchise into a big league team in Chicago, making him the only player in baseball's history to become an owner of a major league team. Before this could happen, he had to make a deal with James Hart, owner of the Chicago Cubs. Hart declared that Commy could never use the word "Chicago" in the team's name, and the home stadium for the new team must be south of 35th street in a remote section of town, far away from the West Side Park, where the Cubbies played. Furthermore, Hart only agreed with creating a second city team because he had past relations with Commy and he thought the new team, or the new American League for that matter, would sink like so many organizations in the past.[14]

Matthew Drew

For once, Commy did what he was told, moving the team to a sketchy ex-cricket field on 39th Street and Princeton, four miles south of the loop, blocks north of the Chicago Union Stockyards—where the stench of dead animals permeated the air. Despite the air's awful smell and land's weeded ruggedness, the location seemed natural to him, since he was a Chicago native, and it was smack dab in the Irish section of the Bridgeport neighborhood. Plus, he knew he could use his father's "friends" in the Irish ward to help him establish cheaper building contracts. He knew it would take a lot to turn the decrepit cricket field into a wooden stadium capable of holding major league events.

For the time being, he settled for a white-washed, medium-sized wooden stadium he named South Side Park. He dreamed that he would one day increase the amount of seats and improve grand stand to accommodate his wealthy associates.

As soon as the unimpressive stadium was ready for play, Commy named his team the "White Stockings" after his favorite childhood team.[15] The Stockings team did not take off as he would have hoped. They lost their opening game on a frigid day on April 21, 1900, by several runs. After opening day, reporters made gray predictions about the Stockings team, as well as the rest of the teams in the newly established American League. Commy had some reservations about his new team as well. He needed to get the most from his average players who came mostly from minor league franchises and disbanded NL teams, but many had promise. For example, one such player William "Dummy" Hoy, a deaf, mostly-mute centerfielder, who stole 32 bases and hit .250 in 1900. The only problem was he was an awful hitter.[16]

Since the team was good at best, Commy had to play around with the team dynamics to make them work as a cohesive unit. He used his fired-up speeches and aggressive coaching techniques to propel the team forward. It would

39

Shadows of Chicago

not take long for the team to work together under their leader. As the team caught fire, the seats in the new stadium filled to capacity and set the stage for the franchise's first American League pennant with a record of 82 wins and 53 losses. After the pennant win, players gave Commy a five-foot bat to mark his retirement from active duty.[17]

The end of the 1900 season gave Commy promise for the future. He had achieved his dream of being owner of a big league team, and now that he developed his fan base he could purchase the big name players needed to nab a World Series title. But then, he knew that to make this possible, he had to drag himself off the field and into the owner's office. This inevitable fact probably weighed on his emotions. He was already tormented by his father's passing that year, and he must have thought about his father's advice: he shouldn't get caught up in such a "frivolous game." Oddly, it was at the time of his father's death that he was no longer that wild player or that fired-up manager; instead, he was now an owner of a formidable major league team. The very position he despised the most.

He could not have fathomed that he would be one of the most remarkable owners in baseball or be involved in the most sensational scandal in baseball history. But he was always a natural at creating a firestorm.

---

[1] Axelson, G.W. *Commy: The Life Story of Charles A. Comiskey.* Chicago: Riley and Lee Company.
[2] *Ibid.*
[3] *Ibid.*
[4] *Ibid.*
[5] *Ibid.*
[6] *Ibid.*
[7] *Ibid.*
[8] As a young pitcher, Comiskey threw mostly fastballs. Some say as he got a little older he began to throw more curves to offset his burned-out arm. He was an excellent pitcher, but there is no way to find out if he was good enough or healthy enough for the big leagues.

[9] Comiskey and his wife had a child that died early on, and had another Lou, that would take on ownership of the White Sox.
[10] Axelson.
[11] *Ibid.*
[12] *Ibid.*
[13] *Ibid.*
[14] Axelson.
[15] The original White Stockings team changed their name to the Orphans. The Orphans were then called the Cubs. The new American league White Stockings changed gradually over time, mostly due to newspapers nicknaming the team the White Sox. It wouldn't be until 1911 that the word "Sox" appeared on a jersey. Also, after the turn of the century, the word "stockings" carried a more feminine meaning.
[16] Lindberg, Richard C. *Total White Sox. The Definitive Enclyclopedia of the Chicago White Sox.* Chicago: Triumph Books.
[17] *Ibid.*

Shadows of Chicago

Chapter 4

BIG JIM

Like Charles Comiskey's father, Jim Horan's parents fled from Ireland during the Potato Famine. In 1850 they survived the journey to Chicago only to learn they now represented the most hated ethnic group among the hundred thousand, half foreign born residents in the city. Patrick Horan chose to ignore typecasts placed on his nationality, working as a laborer on farms just south of his home. Through hard work he earned the respect of others, quickly rising to a cotton broker—a management position trading cotton to Chicago's rising businesses. It was a rare advancement for an Irish immigrant at the time. Patrick Horan's grand endeavors and flair for salesmanship developed into a lifelong lesson for his son Jim.[1]

From the moment Jim was born to Patrick and Ellen on May 10, 1859, people were drawn to his magnetic personality and charm, causing relatives and close friends to nickname him "Sunny Jim."[2] It was his beaming nature and sense of duty that made him a natural for the fire department.

It was ten years after the Great Chicago Fire of 1871, and a long time waiting, when 22-year-old Jim Horan entered his dream job on the Chicago Fire Department. Like any new fire candidate, he had to earn his place among the men. In his case, it started when he was a water boy, the lowest-end job there was. His menial duty was to pump drinking water from a 2,000-foot artesian well into a battered, nozzle-less sprinkler can and then run it back and forth to relieve his company during fires.[3] Often times the men would kick over his can or spit chewing tobacco in the fresh water—a hazing ritual for amusement and to observe how much running their "kid" could endure.[4] The only real objection of their water boy was that he liked to stand too close to the fire, causing the drinking water to get too hot—conduct they probably secretly respected. But no matter how well Jim performed his duty, they would position their charred faces and smoky eyes in front of him, cursing and taunting him to test if the hazing would weaken his knees.[5] All the while, Jim remained confident and genial, seeing the hazing as a stepping stone towards gaining the respect of his men.

    Jim's first opportunity to gain their esteem came at his first fire at Union Stockyards in 1881, when a few of his company members became trapped under a wall of bricks and lumber. As fire and debris hampered rescuers from entering the area where the men lay trapped, onlookers were surprised to see Jim carrying a 100-pound can atop the fallen rubble, intently fighting his way to the imprisoned men. Once he struggled to reach them, he quenched their thirst and allowed them to wash their seared faces until others arrived to help him move the heavy rubble and pull the beaten men to safety.

    Jim's company found an occasion to repay their water boy for his selfless duty. One day, as Jim rode along on the company's fire truck while responding to a fire, the reins slipped from the driver's hands, causing the frantic horses to run wildly through the streets, smashing through a railway gate and narrowly missing a freight train. As the truck continued to swerve and threaten to tip the cab over, Jim climbed between two of the horses, stepped on the pole connecting them and snapped the line on the bit, bringing the truck to a stop.

    Once the truck arrived at the fire, the chief reprimanded Jim for the delay, because blame usually filtered down the ranks to the least senior man. But instead of implicating the driver, he awaited punishment, knowing his water boy position was only probationary and he could easily lose his chance for a dream job on the department. Luckily, Jim's entire company (whether they witnessed the scene or not) approached the chief to expose the true story. Immediately afterward, the chief dropped the charges and expunged the incident from his record, but off the record, Jim's courage would be remembered among the city's firemen.[6]

Soon after tales about Jim caught wind, he was promoted to pipeman on an engine company after only months on the job. His tall, athletic frame and his tireless effort as water boy gained him the nickname "Big Jim"—but the new nickname had more meaning for those who really knew him—many sensed he was passionate enough to create momentous changes for the sprawling city. No one noticed his leadership qualities more than fire department heads, so he was promoted yearly, and in 1893 he made battalion chief with 10 years of service. Although it probably didn't hurt that he was Irish and knew the right people.

Big Jim's progression to battalion chief was partly due to his numerous rescues of civilians and firefighters, but only once he became chief did his daring exploits reach the front page headlines—sensational fire rescue stories rarely involved chiefs, because many of them were busy directing firefighters from outside burning structures or keeping themselves out of the collapse zone—which was typically a distance two times the height of a structure. Big Jim stood out from other chiefs because he was always in the action, fighting side-by-side with his men, making the rescues, regardless if there was a charged hose guiding the way or a teetering wall beside him.

One of his most memorable rescues as battalion chief happened while fighting a fire at a three-story residence. During the first few minutes of the fire, Big Jim and the men already doused the fire and ventilated up to the top of the second floor, and, as it seemed, they were in control of knocking it all down. Once they tried progressing up the stairs to the third floor, however, flames shot through the stairs, impeding their access to the third story and hampering their ability to wash the remaining fire or rescue any remaining civilians. Seeing that most advantageous route to the seat of the fire was out of the question, Big Jim had no choice but to direct the men to hit the third story from the outside, increasing the chances of losing the building, or worse, losing anyone trapped up there.

Portrait of Fire Chief James "Big Jim" Horan at his desk. 1906; Photographer--Chicago Daily News, Inc. Chicago History Museum, #DN-0003653.

Just as his men and he exited the building, he heard onlookers screaming and pointing to a woman trapped above him on a third story window ledge. Smoke and extreme heat caused the woman to dangle hopelessly above the pavement below. Seeing this, he threw off his coat for better agility and scaled up the only ladder available to the third story. Finding the ladder 12-feet too short to reach the woman, he called for his driver, Lieutenant Egan, to climb atop his shoulders. Next, he told Captain William Barker, the smallest of the three, to climb up both Egan and himself. After Barker climbed both Big Jim and Egan, he was easily able to reach the woman and free her from the window ledge, allowing her to slide down the human ladder to safety.[7]

    An equally notable rescue happened a year later when a 38-year-old woman passed out from smoke inhalation on a fourth-floor fire escape of a four-story residence. There was too much smoke on the escape's landing for firemen to risk rescuing the woman, so Big Jim climbed up to the landing while holding his breath.[8] Still without letting smoke enter his lungs, he took his white chief's helmet and used it to break a window. From the narrow opening he placed the woman in a safe room and then maneuvered his large body through the same opening, attempting to avoid shards of glass as he went. Then he put her atop his shoulders and carried her down the four flights of stairs, and, by the time she was carried out the door, she regained consciousness. Just as she came to and hugged Big Jim, the firemen working above them threw a feather mattress off the balcony. The mattress broke on the escape, causing feathers to snow down on them and the spectators who had watched the rescue take place.[9]

    Needless to say, the reporters ate the story up, but when they rushed to the young chief to inquire about the sensational rescue he broke into his distinctive spiel: "Horan's no hero. He's just a fireman and it's all in a day's work. Never mind about those honorable mentions. There's a lot of bunk in it anyway, and let's forget about it." Anytime he was asked to talk about his experiences he would talk in the third person, either because he was modest (typical of any stoic Irishmen) or he didn't like the hullabaloo. Regardless, his men got such a kick out of his third-person rants they mocked him all over the city, and all in good fun.

Shadows of Chicago

As the public became more and more engrossed with the young battalion chief, reporters began to pose questions about his romantic life. He felt compelled to hide his courtships from the public eye because he was a widower—his wife had died a few years before of unknown causes, leaving him with two adult children. Besides that, he was a church-going Catholic, so it wasn't something he would talk about.

But it wasn't long before he gave up the public façade. This ended when he met Margaret Mahoney, a beautiful young secretary to the First Fire Marshal. Margaret was accustomed to high-ranking officers flirting with her at the city hall office, but it wasn't until she got to know Big Jim that she realized she met a man who encompassed the qualities she desired: someone who's confident and true to others. Similarly, he admired Margaret's strength and compassion and, most importantly, she seemed willing to accept his precarious approach to the chief's position.

After only a couple months together, the couple married in 1903, and soon had two children of their own. Big Jim confidently spoke about his new wife to the public, referring to her only as "Mrs. Horan." He was using a hackneyed expression from Ireland, where wives were often referred to as "the missus." People closest to Big Jim and Margaret said they appeared to be happy together. But as they openly displayed their affection for one another, deep down the both must have considered the risks he took and that the further he advanced in the fire department the more he would be absent from home. Big Jim also knew he would have to spend more time away from his family to make the improvements he wanted in the fire department, and the only way this could happen would be if he moved up to the highest position.

Matthew Drew

---

[1] Rice, John. *Research Data, 1910 Stockyards Fire,* November 28, 2001.

[2] *Ibid.*

[3] Kolomay, Marion. *Account of the Great Stockyard Fire*

[4] Chewing tobacco was used as a filter to decrease the amount of smoke into the lungs. The nickname "kid" referred to a new fire candidate, regardless of age. The name stayed with the new firefighter until he proves his abilities and/or a new firefighter with less seniority enters the firehouse.

[5] "Smoky eyes" was slang for the red, soot-tearing eyes from excessive smoke.

[6] Kolomay.

[7] Rice.

[8] The Self Contained Breathing Apparatus (SCBA) was not invented for another half a century.

[9] Kolomay.

Shadows of Chicago

Chapter 5

FREDDY

When he was a child, Fred Busse looked up to older kids like Horan and Comiskey, but unlike them, it was his nature to draw attention away from himself. If his independence was threatened, it was often his way to strike back, usually with his fists. Oddly, his need for solitude carried on into politics, where he would rarely talk about his life to the public and barely to the people whom he knew best.

Because of this, little is known about his early family life, except that he was born to German immigrant parents on March 3, 1866 in Chicago. His father, Gustave, was a Civil War hero, a Union captain serving at Shiloh. After the war, Gustave ran a small hardware store where he taught his son Fred the ins and outs of running a small business. Fred adopted his father's business sense and, later in life, like his father, became an avid supporter of the Republican Party.

However, politics never seemed to be his natural calling, but business was. At a young age, Fred proved to be an excellent wheeler and dealer, moving from his father's hardware business to the coal business, eventually becoming president of the Busse Coal Company. He spent his free time boozing with other big businessmen, and occasionally throwing a punch or two to settle an argument. It was never Fred's way to settle scores by talking it out; instead, he had reserved a rock-hard demeanor until he was pushed too far. For instance, one time when he was teased during a card game at the Illinois Athletic Club (once his favorite hangout), he used his connections to close the place down.[1] His knee-jerk response would cost him a powerful ally in the Republican Party, Big Bill Thompson—who

51

would become longtime Chicago mayor and a proud supporter of the city's underworld. Suffice it to say, Fred's "I'll-show-you" approach didn't make him many friends.

Oddly enough, his less-than-personable manner did not prevent him from political advancement. To his supporters he was a highly-regarded businessman who had a high-degree of common sense and was sharp as a tack. To some of his most ardent supporters he was known as the fairest man in politics.[2]

In 1891, at 25-years-old, the portly Busse entered politics as clerk of North Chicago. It was never his intention of enter the politics to improve the city. Rather, politics was just another business venture, a sure way to keep money in his pockets. So after a few years as clerk, he moved on to state politics. He started off at the Illinois House of Representatives for a couple terms, served four years as senator, and then was elected state treasurer in 1902. As treasurer he developed a friendship with President Theodore Roosevelt, who helped him become postmaster of Chicago in 1905. As postmaster, Busse brushed shoulders with the big dogs in the Republican Party, while the common people in Chicago knew nothing about him, especially the Democrats.

Because he was uncontroversial and seemingly uncorrupted by the politics of the day, Chicago Republicans thought he would make an ideal candidate for mayor in 1907. More importantly, he would make a good puppet, perfect for protecting the party's personal interests. His most appealing aspect to his party was that he was a German, a sure way to deter many ethnic voters away from the Democrats.[3]

Contrary to what many believed, Busse was neither new to machine politics nor was he beyond political corruption. The fact was he was not naive to vote-buying. He spent many years as political boss of the North Side faction of the Republican Party, helping his connections get elected. Additionally, he associated with gangsters, like Christian "Barney" Bertsche, a member of the North Side gang in charge of running brothels and illegal gambling hideouts.[4] There's little doubt that Fred turned a blind eye to the goings-on in his ward.[5]

At the time, the press knew nothing about his association with the city's criminal element, so prior to Chicago's mayoral election of 1907, reporters never felt much of a need to fire tough questions at him. To them, Busse was a lame-duck candidate with nothing controversial to say. Many gave up because they were sick of hearing his short, vague comments. The few reporters who ventured to press him on key issues had trouble finding him. They ventured so far as to try to catch him at home, where he was still living with his parents (he wouldn't move out until he was 42-years-old). Newspaper accounts told amusing stories of his mother fighting off reporters when they tried to get him out of his house to answer questions. When Fred wasn't at his parents' home, he hanging out with his cast of shady characters at J.C. Murphy's saloon on Clark Street and North Avenue—soon reporters were calling him the "saloon-keepers politician" in the papers—and outside the papers amongst themselves they called him "Fat Freddy."[6]

As reporters let off Busse because they were bored with his antics, his campaign staff was busy devising a slick trick to gain the mayor's seat. His staff knew this mayoral election was important, because Chicago, like the rest of the nation, was in the midst of the Progressive Era, a time of great political upheaval. The biggest issues of time were modernization, municipal reform, and social reform.[7]

Chicago, more than any other city at the time, was in the throes of social reform. People were sick of political corruption, the school system, and the mass transit system. Many of the problems were blamed on the incumbent mayor, Edward Dunne. In addition, a growing number of

Shadows of Chicago

people accused Dunne of vote-buying and dirty machine politics, turning many of his followers away from him. Despite this, he was a crafty machine politician and would still destroy Busse in the polls. Plus, the Republicans hadn't won an election in over a decade. Busse needed something big to happen if he wanted to get the mayoral seat.[8]

*   *   *   *

Fred Busse was alive, but unconscious laying in his blood and a deep pool of ice cold water. As he slept, his fat, limp body was hurled several feet from his bed at midnight and jammed into the narrow passageway near his bathroom. Cold water flowed into his lungs, causing asphyxiation. This would kill him if he didn't die first from a laceration close to his major artery in his thigh. Along with his life threatening injuries, much of his body was badly bruised.

He lay wounded and unconscious for an hour before help arrived. Before that he was sleeping comfortably in his first-class Pullman sleeping car. He was in Washington on post-office business with President Theodore Roosevelt and was returning to Chicago to give speeches for a mayoral race—something he dreaded more than anything.

On February 21, 1907, the train left New York about 3:55 p.m., carrying a combination baggage-buffet car, two Pullman passenger cars, and a compartment observation car, along with 70 souls. At about midnight, as the train continued on from Philadelphia, the engineer tried to make up lost time by pushing the steam engine to its limits along a farmland expanse between Altoona and Johnstown, Pennsylvania. Just as the engine struggled to reach a curve towards the summit of a hill, a brake beam on the second Pullman car jerked loose, possibly due to the severe cold, which caused one of the bolts to spring loose at the high rate of speed. This forced the first car from the track and then the last three cars were thrown from the rails, causing the couplings between the combination car and the first Pullman to break. The engine bolted free from the steel rails, plowing through the frozen ground for 500 feet, mowing down telegraph poles along the way. Meanwhile, the three rear cars slid down the embankment into the shallow part of the Conemaugh River. If the river was deeper, unfrozen, or if cars would have rolled, just about every passenger, including Busse, would have been slaughtered instantly.[9]

It took a relief train of rescuers about an hour to reach Busse and the other wounded passengers, and judging from the wreck, they expected the worst. To their astonishment, only 40 people were injured a few, like Busse, hurt seriously. When rescuers found him, they thought he wasn't going to make it, but once he was brought to the hospital, doctors were able to treat his punctured left lung, severe lacerations, and broken collar bone. He also had two black-and-blue eyes and fractured ribs. All his wounds were expected to heal over time.[10]

No one could have guessed that the horrible train accident would turn out to be the most opportune event in Busse's political career. Since the doctors ordered him to get bed rest, this freed him from making campaign speeches—something he avoided doing the entire mayoral campaign of 1907. From his bed he told reporters otherwise, telling them how angered he was that he could not make any campaign appearances at this time.

With Busse confined to his bed, his Republican followers were now able to turn the election in his favor. So, as Busse bed-rested from the train wreck, the Republican Party assumed control of the dirty mayoral election. First they called on their friends at *The Chicago Tribune* to create sensational stories about the accident, depicting Busse as a helpless man, who, if not confined to his bed, would be out their fighting for the rights of the people. The

Shadows of Chicago

Page 1 headlines read, "Busse a Fighter; Credit to City," and "Busse's Career in Politics: Product of Chicago and Known as a Man Who Does Things—Influence For Harmony." The *Trib* went so far as devise a cartoon of Busse reading in his bed while Mayor Dunne aids threw buckets of mud on him.[11]

As the *Trib* ridiculed Dunne, his Republican campaign preached that Busse was a champion of the sick and poor and that he would be the best mayor to improve educational institutions throughout the city. That was just enough bull to help Busse win the mayor's seat with only a little over 13,000 votes.

Now as mayor, and the supposed champion of social reform, would he have the guts to shut down the vice in the First Ward?

---

[1] Mark, Norman. *Mayors Madams & Madmen*. Chicago: Chicago Review Press, 1979.

[2] "Death Closes Varied Career of Fred Busse," *Chicago Daily Tribune,* July 10, 1914.

[3] Flanagan, Maureen A. "Fred Busse: A Silent Mayor in Turbulent Times." *The Mayors: the Chicago Political Tradition*. Carbondale: Southern Illinois University Press, 1995.

[4] Christian "Barney" Bertsche would eventually lose his prostitution enterprise to Al Capone. He was responsible for killing a detective and two cops shortly before Busse took office in 1907.

[5] Mark.

[6] Abbott, Karen. *Sin in the Second City. Madams, Ministers, Playboys and the Battle for America's Soul*. New York: Random House, 2007.

[7] *Ibid*.

[8] *Ibid*.

[9] "18-Hour Flyer Goes Into River; Fred Busse Hurt," *Chicago Daily Tribune,* February 23, 1907.

[10] *Ibid*.

[11] Flanagan.

Chapter 6

THE CURSED FIRST WARD

The story of the infamous First Ward began on a summer's day in 1812. Captain Billy Wells, accompanied by 30 of his fellow Miami Indians, arrived at Fort Dearborn. Wells, a white man, was kidnapped by the Miami while living in Kentucky. Instead of escaping from his captors, he decided to adopt their language and their ways, either because he wished to learn from his adopted family or he had a wicked case of Stockholm's Syndrome. Either way, under the brave Chief Little Turtle, he increased his hunting and fighting skills like never before. Soon the Miami tribe became impressed with their strong white brother and found him to be a great benefit to their tribe, so he was quickly accepted and given the name Apekonit, or "Carrot-top," for his striking red hair—a trait most Miami had never seen.

Billy Wells gained so much mythical notoriety throughout the Northwest Territory that his niece Rebekah, who was married to Captain Nathan Heald, leader of the garrison at Fort Dearborn, gave him the impossible task of protecting them from the angered Pottawattamie Natives. The Pottawatomie became enraged because Captain Heald reneged on his promises of barrels of whiskey and ammunition to their people. Heald's fateful decision put everyone, including women and children, in immediate danger, and Wells, more than anyone, knew that an attack was coming. So much so, that he painted his face black, a mark of eminent death.

Captain Wells and his 30 Miami led Fort Dearborn's garrison across the prairie, many hoping that the Pottawatomie would just let them pass unscathed until they reached a safe haven at an American-friendly outpost to the

Shadows of Chicago

East. As fate would have it, they would not travel much further than the walls of the fort, for at what is now Michigan and Roosevelt, a one-sided battle ensued. Although what happened next is still debated, the fact was that Wells' 30 Miami escorts fled, leaving him to fight off hoards of attackers with 40-something men.

Wells and the men fought bravely through the front line of the attackers. Meanwhile, as they fought against impossible odds, a few rogue Indians started hacking away at white women and children (they were supposedly exiled from the tribe for this). After seeing this, several soldiers back-tracked to protect them. Wells, on the other hand, progressed further through the enemy lines, killing and maiming everything in his path (some say he killed Indian women and children as well). In the midst of his fury, Wells was surrounded, held, and beheaded, and, to the surprise of many, his heart torn out and his blood drunk to acquire his bravery.

The fight would end soon after. On the blood-drenched field 25 regular soldiers, 12 militiamen, two women, 12 children, and 15 Pottawatomie died—many more died soon after. It would be almost 20 years later that white settlers would find the bleached bones of those killed.[1]

Many were quick to dub the conflict "The Fort Dearborn Massacre" without considering both the white and the Indian accounts. But even considering all accounts, the only thing that can be ascertained for sure is that it was a deal that went horribly wrong. And ironically, on the same six-square miles of land of Captain Heald's false promises and the bloody conflict, Chicago's notorious First Ward would arise, the site of rotten politically-backed or mafia-based crimes that would harm and kill many innocent people for more than a century.

*   *   *   *

Matthew Drew

The land on which the First Ward originated was ceded to white settlers on August 18, 1835, at the south branch of the Chicago River. The Pottawatomie and other tribes did their final dance, wailing, and striking of their tomahawks at invisible enemies—most likely directed at the new white settlers. The leering white settlers who witnessed the dance said it looked as if they placed a curse on the land.[2]

The first settlers would not have disagreed; it seemed to all that the land was unsuitable for living. It reeked of the native garlic plants and was nearly impossible to farm because it was barely above river level, so wherever the people walked, seeded, plowed, or tried to do anything, they did so in the mud.[3] It was fitting that the locals nicknamed the area "Mudtown," and even sometimes just "Mudhole." Legend has it that once a man was seen with only his head sticking out of the mud. When someone asked if he needed help, the man answered, "No thanks. I have a horse under me."[4]

The settlers who were lucky to grow enough food in the mud still had to survive the ice-cold winters and the swarms of malaria-spreading insects during the steamy summers. Nevertheless, it wouldn't take long for the people of the area to build a great city on the God-forsaken land.

Even though progress was halted temporally after The Great Chicago Fire, the First Ward would be the first area to rise again from the ashes, developing the swankest, proudest buildings in the nation. Some of the best architects in the world developed gorgeous buildings along Michigan Avenue. The area boasted the most decorative mansions, first-rate hotels, theaters, and the tallest buildings of the time. This brought visitors and people with money to the city, where they would find the best restaurants, operas, a symphony orchestra, and giant department stores. Big business was equally drawn to the city, and all along LaSalle Street the nation's biggest business centers grew.

Shadows of Chicago

Despite the impressive features of the First Ward's rising infrastructure, it was just a façade for where the big-time money was generated. Only blocks away from where some nice couple might go to a eat a four-star dinner, attend one of the best plays, or take a late-night stroll gazing at the brilliant architecture, was the Levee, a place where they could fall victim to a cast of thousands of pickpocketers, rapists, and gangsters.[5]

The Levee extended from Wabash to Clark and from 18th to 22nd streets. Through the entire Levee's history, naive visitors who mistakenly ventured into the Levee would by the end of the night be beat-up, wallets depleted—or if they met up with someone like the infamous bartender Mickey Finn, they would be unknowingly slipped a drug and then taken for everything they came with.

Others, who were willing participants, found that the Levee could satisfy any lust they had. In *Wicked City*, Curt Johnson described it best: "In the Levee could be found debauchery to satisfy every man's heart's desire: faro joints, dice joints, policy stations, gyp auctions, arcades, hock shops, opium dens, peep shows, dance halls, plain and concert saloons, burlesque houses, and brothels to cater to every taste at rates scaled to every bill clip or coin purse." Some of the triple-X-rated brothels went well beyond the norm (even for them), including animals and underage prostitutes.[6]

The wickedest brothels were found at Bed Bug Row—a group of run-down shanties—bed bugs were probably the least hazardous thing they'd catch there. If customers wanted more "refined sex" they went to the other side of Wabash to The Everleigh Club, a brothel the rest of the Levee called "Mama and Papa Fucking." Once there, while patrons waited for one of the well-rounded madams, they sat in one of the 12 large reception parlors, decorated with gold, copper and silver, and could sample a rare classic from the library, all the while listening to one of the three

Matthew Drew

four-piece orchestras. Karen Abbot, in *Sin in the Second City: Madams, Ministers, Playboys and the Battle for America's Soul,* explained, "[The brothel] had a large and sumptuous dining room, decorated, a replica of the Pullman Palace Car buffet, rich carpets, gold plated spittoons, marble statuary and imported oil painting, hardwood floors of rare woods in mosaic patterns, gold bathtub and shower, perfumed aphrodisiac spray. Every room had a fountain which regularly jetted perfume into the air. It employed 15 to 25 of the finest chefs and maids in the nation. On special occasions they would open boxes of butterflies. An envious rival madam remarked 'No man for sure is going to forget he got his balls fanned by a butterfly at the Everleigh Club.'"

The Everleigh Club's décor went a little overboard, but there was no denying that it was the most luxurious brothel ever created. The creative work of madam-sisters Minna and Ada Everleigh paid off, but it didn't happen overnight. The Everleighs ran a second-rate prostitution ring in Omaha, Nebraska. Using the cash they made there, and a $35,000 they supposedly inherited from their father, they moved to Chicago to build the swankest brothel in the world. On Feburary 1, 1900, the sisters spent just about every penny on a three-story brownstone at 21st and South Dearborn with all the most over-the-top furnishings.[7]

From Everleigh Club's inception, the main objective was to provide luxury, because most visitors would come for the ambiance and to boast, "Hey, you wouldn't believe what it looked like in there." Its secondary objective was to provide the best girls around. In the Everleigh's biography by Charles Washburn, *Come Into My Parlor,* he explains that only the prettiest, well-mannered girls were chosen and they were given specific rules of behavior. The girls were rounded up and Ada Everleigh would explain, "The Everleigh Club is not for the rough element, the clerk on a holiday, or a man without a checkbook. Your youth and beauty are all you have. Preserve it. Stay respectable by all means....To get in, a girl must have a pretty face and figure,

61

must be in perfect health, and must look well in evening clothes."8

The fee for the best girls around ran from $150 to $1000, plus tip. For more than a decade some would gross about $2000, sometimes $5,000 a night. Some would even make a $125,000 a year from the big-money patrons, including some of the most famous people at the turn of the century: poet Edgar Lee Masters, actor John Barrymore, boxer "Gentleman" Jim Corbett, the famous industrialist John "Bet-a-Million" Gates, the brother of Kaiser Wilhelm II, an entire U. S. Congressional Committee, and Ring Lardner (one of the sports columnists to break the Black Sox scandal).9 Besides the famous personalities, many of the country's financial elite, including members of the meat-packing monopoly, were also visitors to the club.

There was also a strict policy for men. They were expected to have a card of introduction and were expected to be on their best behavior, because the Everleigh sisters knew that to have the best-run brothel they had to keep out the trouble. This in turn would attract the most elite, including the politicians who would keep the show running.

Also, to keep their business afloat they needed the best protection. Protection was paid to a white-suited, jewelry-flashing Italian immigrant named Giacomo "Big Jim" Colosimo. With his cheesy mustached grin he would enter Everleigh Club yelling, "Salute! Buon giorno!," and then the sisters would pay him a weekly allowance for protection. In turn, as a sign of friendship, Colosimo would prepare a spaghetti dinner on Sunday evenings at the club. What seemed a good deed was probably done so he could sample some of the club's best girls. Beautiful women became such a passion of his he would one day run about 200 brothels of his own.10

Compared to what he'd become, Colosimo, at the time, was still small potatoes. During the Everleigh Club's first years, he was just a precinct captain and bagman. As the club's muscle, it was his duty to collect money, occasionally roughing up some and making others disappear, and then bringing the money to the Levee's First Ward political leaders, Aldermen "Bathhouse John" Coughlin and "Hinky-Dink" Kenna, known to all as the "Lords of the Levee." Their title was a little misleading, because Bathhouse and Hinky-Dink's power was not limited to Levee or the First Ward. Their power extended to the city, county, state, and federal offices. Just about everyone was on their payroll, so no one could investigate their illicit activities.

They made a formidable team, but that didn't mean they were alike. Bathhouse was a 250-pound loud goof, who often sported flamboyant clothing like multi-colored waistcoats and for everyone's amusement a baby blue bathing suit with red polka dots. He published peculiar poetry and songs in the papers (that he had no problem reciting in public), and, after a few drinks, he was guaranteed to hurl bottles and furniture in the air, or fight just about anybody. People who didn't know him said he was a simple-minded buffoon (perhaps that's way he liked it), but that was far from the truth. Bathhouse ran an agency that took care of the insurance on the brothels in the Levee and for the ward's illegal businesses. On top of that, he owned half the interest in the one supply house that monopolized all food and liquor in the Levee.[11]

By the looks of things, Bathhouse's partner "Hinky-Dink" Kenna was quite the opposite. Hinky-Dink was 5-foot-4 with a toothpick frame, and there was nothing gaudy about his appearance, except that he sported a curly, upturned mustache, like the bartenders of old. His manner was even less unassuming: he was meek, nearly-silent, and shrewd. It was in back rooms of the saloons and brothels that he was a force to be reckoned with. If you wanted something from him, you'd shut up, and he'd do all the talking. He conducted most of his business at his saloon, The Workingman's Exchange on Clark and Van Buren streets. The saloon boasted that it was the longest bar in the world (100 feet) and the "The Largest and Coolest Schooner of Beer in the City." Hinky-Dink hired out thugs to round up as many patrons as possible, including the insane, criminals, drifters, and homeless (even if they were lying in piss and vomit) and then drag them into the saloon.[12]

When the down-and-out arrived, they were treated to a pint of beer and the best free lunch anywhere for only five cents. If they didn't have the money, Hinky-Dink would get them a job; if they had trouble with the police, he'd get them off; if they were homeless, he'd put them up in his sleazy hotel he had above the bar—the stay included a bucket of leftover wine, booze and stale beer called "a rub of the brush."

In return for Hinky-Dink's "goodwill" they had to cast their vote for him and anyone else he wanted—no questions asked. On Election Day, when his so-called supporters went out to the polling places in the First Ward, they carried with them pre-marked ballots. Once the marked ballots were deposited in the ballot box, the blank ballot received upon entering the polling place was brought back for a reward of 50 cents. The blank ballots were newly-marked and the procedure was done again at a different polling place. Quite fittingly, on Election Day the motto of the Democratic Party in the First Ward was "Vote early and often."[13]

Despite Hinky-Dink's impressive system, and the 600 or so followers in his saloon on election eve, it still wasn't the sizable gathering he felt he needed to secure a victory. To lock an election win and fill his greedy, little pockets, he also ran the infamous First Ward Ball. Each year starting in 1897, just before Election Day, the First Ward Ball took place, gathering some 15,000 people to partake in the wildest political shindig in the nation, or what the Illinois Crime Survey termed the "annual underworld orgy." Before the festivities began, Bathhouse, the grand marshal of the ball, after making his rounds to check to see if all the guests were their supporters (escorted by two police officers) began the ball with a poem: "On with this dance/ Let the orgy be perfectly proper/ Don't drink, smoke or spit on the floor/ And say keep your eye on the copper." Just seconds after the toast, the place went up for grabs.[14]

A reporter for *The Chicago Herald* said the 1907 First Ward Ball featured women in "tawdry costumes of Egyptian dancers, Indian maidens, geisha girls and gypsies—all were abbreviated skirts when any were worn. The parties went until 3 a.m., men and women passed out on the doors, tables and chairs, snored and gasped." Among the rabble-rousers were police, judges, and politicians, and at the center of it all was Bathhouse, who was throwing fists, tables, and chairs, and fondling unwilling girls. Actually, any woman who entered the ball was there for the taking.[15]

Many years later, reporting on vice and corruption in Chicago, the Illinois Crime Survey described the yearly ritual as "the annual underworld orgy, given by Alderman Michael Kenna ('Hinky Dink') and Alderman John Coughlin ('Bathhouse John'), bosses of the First Ward, for the purpose of retaining control of prostitutes and criminals of the First Ward Levee for political purposes and for political funds."[16]

After every First Ward Ball, Hinky-Dink and Bathhouse's aldermanic reelection was safe and sound along with their protection, not to mention the upwards of $50,000 they brought in from each of the parties. The First Ward Ball would keep rolling from year to year, unless Mayor Busse would do something about it.

---

[1] Geoffrey Johnson, "The True Story of the Deadly Encounter at Fort Dearborn," *Chicago*, December 2009.

Shadows of Chicago

² Mark, Norman. *Mayors Madams & Madmen*. Chicago: Chicago Review Press, 1979.

³ Miami Native Americans named Chicago after the native garlic plant. The word Chicago means "wild onion" –when translated by the Pottawatomie—the next tribe that inherited the land.

⁴ Cronon, William. *Nature's Metropolis: Chicago and the Great West*. New York: W.W. Norton & Company, 1995.

⁵ Johnson, Curt. *Wicked City. Chicago: From Kenna to Capone*. December Press. 1994.

⁶ *Ibid.*

⁷ Abbott, Karen. *Sin in the Second City. Madams, Ministers, Playboys and the Battle for America's Soul*. New York: Random House, 2007.

⁸ *Ibid.*

⁹ Johnson.

¹⁰ Johnson.

¹¹ Mark, Norman. *Mayors Madams & Madmen*. Chicago: Chicago Review Press, 1979.

¹² Abbott.

¹³ Mark.

¹⁴ Abbott.

¹⁵ *Ibid.*

¹⁶ "The Illinois Crime Survey," *Illinois Association for Criminal Justice,* Chicago: Illinois Association for Criminal Justice, 1929.

Chapter 7

THE HITLESS WONDERS

After the 1900 pennant-winning season and onwards, Comiskey was done skittering along the bench, hollering at umpires, and sparking-up his fellow players. All that fired-up energy he had on the playing field was now bottled up, reserved for storming the major league teams. Every home game, through his heavy wire screen below the stands, he ogled each player's strengths as well as every lost opportunity. When he wasn't glued to the game, he was in his office devising inventive ways of winning.

When his players were summoned to his office, he was known as Mr. Comiskey. Only the few who knew him during his wild playing days referred to him as Commy. To everybody else he was known as the "Old Roman" for his pronounced hooked nose. This was also because he packed on a few pounds, moved a little slower, showed more and more signs of graying hair, and wore a gray wide-brimmed hat like the politicians of the day. His outward appearance changed as well as did his outlook on the team's future. He took ownership of the team more seriously than he ever had in the past. But one thing never changed, he was determined to win at any cost.

In the 1901 season, now that Comiskey and American League president Ban Johnson were able to sever ties with the National Agreement, the AL was able to purchase top players from the National League. For Comiskey and Johnson their shared dream of making a formidable American League was reality, but their friendship would suffer because the two disagreed on the future of the league. Comiskey longed for the eventual take over the NL, while Johnson favored ongoing competition

Shadows of Chicago

between the two leagues. Their differing opinions set a stage for a feud that would last their entire lives.[1]

While Johnson tried to make nice with the NL owners, to the dismay NL owners, as soon as the 1901 season was about to start, Comiskey plucked great players away from them, particularly from the Cubs' (at the time called the Orphans) organization. Right away, he signed Cubs star pitcher Clark Griffith to be player/manager for the team. Griffith in turn talked fellow pitcher Nixey Callahan and infielder Sam Mertes into joining the White Sox (called the White Stockings at the time) as well. Two other big-time purchases were Fielder Jones from the Dodgers and Billy Sullivan from the Braves.[2]

Comiskey spent a fortune on the players to get the team started in the right direction. Even with the purchase of big-name players, NL owners still assumed the White Sox didn't have a chance at a pennant, as well as the rest of the AL teams. Furthermore, the NL still considered the AL a passing fad that would never catch on with the fans because they would never surpass the NL's caliber on the field.

Cubs president James Hart was especially vocal about this opinion of the Sox organization. Before the 1901 season even started, Hart remarked, "They may talk all they want, about the city supporting two teams, but they are mistaken. Chicago can only support one Chicago club!" The Sox couldn't prove Hart any more wrong. At the end of the 1901 season the Sox finished first in the league and pulled in a league-shattering 354,350 fans, while the Cubs placed sixth in the NL and brought in 205,071 fans.[3]

The Southsiders were overwhelmed with their fresh new team. They came in droves to see the team's fast base running, superior pitching, and thrilling defensive play. Even though the team struggled at the plate, fans knew they were in for a surprise every game, so crowds began to over-pack the South Side Park—reminiscent of Commy's playing days. The tiny park became so overwhelmed that in the last home game of the year, on September 15, the Sox hauled in a crowd of 18,000. The bursting of fans in the already crowded outfield caused umpires to call every hit into the roaring crowd a ground-rule triple.[4] To add to the excitement the Sox swept the Brewers in a 9-4 win for the pennant.[5]

Reporters ate up the hoopla around Comiskey and the new Sox team. They were especially amazed at Comiskey's ability to tear players away from the NL teams. To the outrage of the NL owners, reporters called teams in the NL the "tattered remnants" of the major leagues.[6]

NL owners were so angered they would not consider a postseason series for the White Sox, despite the team's capture of the AL pennant. In actuality, the AL was not the only one guilty of stealing players. NL also capitalized on every opportunity to snag the AL's talent and had more money and resources to do so. What became of it all was an all-out war by the end of the 1901 season.

Neither the AL nor the NL owners budged on reaching any kind of agreement. For the time being Comiskey and Ban Johnson worked together to make the American League a long-lasting enterprise and they didn't want to be pushed around by the National League. However, as Ban was preparing a truce, Comiskey wanted to continue to make the NL teams a group of "tattered remnants."[7]

Their arguments would boil over on May 1, 1906 when Comiskey moved out of Ban's office, nearly breaking apart the American League.

* * * *

In 1906, now that the trade war had ended for three years and there seemed to be a pact between the National and American leagues, every owner from both sides of the fence seemed to be at peace, except Comiskey, who gritted his teeth. The only way Comiskey was able to bear the two-league arrangement was because the AL was now allowed to play NL in the World Series.

For him, the Series crown was just within reach. For the past four years he toyed with the players' lineup and always kept a pennant-threatening team, even though every year they struggled at the plate. The best thing he had going was his new manager, Fielder Jones—his star hitter and center fielder since the 1901 pennant. Fielder, like Comiskey in his prime, hated losing and was great at making the most out of mediocrity—it was almost as if Comiskey channeled his fired-up spirit into Jones. Comiskey used Jones as a medium to reach out to the players on the field, but never interfered with the manager-player relationship. Rather, he let Jones capitalize on the team's lightning speed and unyielding defense. Comiskey's biographer G.W. Axelson said, "Given the slimmest kind of opening, a 100 percent defense would be necessary to keep the Sox from trundling the winning run over the plate. Their own defense was nigh perfect. On the offense the slogan was to get on the bases by hook or crook and 'to claim everything.'"[8]

Probably due to the Sox's aggressive play by the end of the first half of the 1906 season, the players were losing steam, triggering possible season-ending injuries. To restore the team for the second half of the season, Comiskey called on an expert in physical conditioning, athletic director Hiram "Doc" Connibear. The Doc brought back the team to their previous magic potential.[9] During the month of August, they had a 19-game-win streak which tied for second longest in AL history—and fourth in majors since 1900.[10]

Throughout the remainder of the 1906 season, the Sox stayed in first place in the AL, pulling out wins through the narrowest of margins. Most wins were due to walks, sacrifice hits, or stretched base running. Unbelievably, the White Sox led the league in walks (453), sacrifices (227), hit basemen (51), and was third in stolen bases. Rarely ever were wins due to great hitting. By the end of the season they batted a collected average of .230, last place among the AL's eight teams. Across the board they were last in every hitting category, atypical of any winning ball club. This is probably how they inherited the nickname "the hitless wonders."[11]

No other "hitless wonder" made more of a sensation than veteran catcher Billy Sullivan. Despite a record number of hitless games every season, his distinctive work behind the plate would revolutionize baseball forever. Throughout the majors, it was typical for catchers to stand 20 feet behind the batter to avoid being cracked by a bat or foul ball—the added distance from home plate made it especially difficult to throw out a man at second or third—this accounted for over 200 stolen bases in a season. In order to place his body closer to the plate, Sullivan developed his own "armor," complete with heavy chest guard, mask and leg covering.[12] With his shielded body he crouched right behind the batter. Imagine the look on the face of the first batter to see this.[13]

Fans were excited to watch the rest of "the hitless wonders" reach for any base and score on every opportunity. The fans roared like never before and were getting a wild reputation of their own, often fighting in the stands or charging the field to holler at umpires. A writer for the *Chicago Daily Tribune* adds, "The pikers who crowd into the first-base bleachers and bet nickels on the innings then roast player or umpire, or hurl bottles at them when they lose, are responsible for the reputation Chicago has of being the toughest town in either Major League circuit."

The most boisterous fans had a lot to celebrate as their Sox met in a sensational race for the pennant with the Yankees, Athletics, and Indians. The Athletics and Indians dropped out of race in early September, leaving behind the White Sox to fight the Yanks for the AL pennant. During the final week of the battle, the White Sox won the pennant by the Yanks splitting a double-header against the Athletics.[14]

Not only were they AL pennant winners, they were about to play their crosstown rivals in the World Series, the Chicago Cubs. The Cubs were possibly the best team in baseball's history. Their coach, Frank Chance, led the team to whopping 116-36 season.[15] The Sox were 93-58. Not a bad record for division leaders, but they were the clear underdogs against the mighty Cubs organization. Comiskey and manager Fielder Jones were mindful of the Cubs's powerhouse offense. On the other hand, they thought they might be able to take advantage of the Cubs's less-than-perfect pitching staff.[16]

The White Sox team's only noticeable edge was their excellent pitching staff, which set a major league record for the most shutouts in a season with 32. As far as the rest of the "hitless wonders," they were expected to have difficulty capitalizing on Cubs' misplays. On the other side of town, the Cubs had command of their fielding, measured up to the Sox's physical ability, and won 55 of their last 63 games. Hugh Fullerton, a *Chicago Daily Tribune* reporter, said, "The fearsome Cubs were to provide the opposition in a remarkable White Sox showdown that was shaping up to be war to the finish between the South Side Davids and the West Side Goliaths." Writers around the country considered the Cubs/Sox series the biggest mismatch in the history of baseball, and, expectedly, the line on the game was 3-1 in favor of the Cubs. Even the best Sox fans, thought they didn't have a prayer in the world. But, Comiskey did.

With the announcement of the all-Chicago World Series came a maddening scramble to find tickets or find a place to hear the game, since radio and television were just of a dream of the future. For those who couldn't get the hottest ticket in Chicago, there were auditoriums located on both sides of the city, for fans to hear the (delayed) play by play from announcers receiving the news by telegraph. In

The White Sox Journal John Snyder described the atmosphere of the crosstown rivalry: "The city was at a virtual standstill for six days in which the two clubs battled for the world title. Two teenage fans, desperate for money so they could buy tickets from scalpers, held up a grocery store. City Alderman Charles Martin, a White Sox fan, was arrested after brawling with a drunken Cubs supporter."[17]

Fans from each side of the city, who were lucky enough to score the hottest ticket in town, each got a chance to watch the game from their home turf. Host fields for the games alternated between the Cubs' West Side Grounds and the White Sox's South Side Park. To the amazement of both fans, the White Sox claimed the World Series title from the highly favored Cubs, winning four games to two. Equally astonishing, the Sox captured the Chicago World Series in game six in front of 19,249 fans at South Side Park.

Many people attributed the Cubs's World Series loss to their poor pitching and fielding, and the Sox again proved to be "the hitless wonders," having batted a record low of .198 in the Series. Yet third basemen George Rohe came through for the team, hitting .333 with seven hits, consisting of a double and two triples—all at the most opportune moments in the games. As a result, Rohe was celebrated as the hero of the series by his fellow players as well as his fans, and praised highly by one who tended to give praise lightly, Charles Comiskey. As a consequence of helping boost the team to victory, Comiskey declared, "Whatever George Rohe may do from now on, he's signed on for life with me!" Then, quite comically, after Rohe hit .213 the following season, Comiskey canned him from the team.[18]

Already Comiskey was seen as a hard loser, but after the 1906 World Series victory, he was proved to be a bit of a hard winner as well. For example, of the $106,550 the 1906 team generated, he gave Fielder Jones only $15,000 to be shared among the players. But to Comiskey's credit, he had

Shadows of Chicago

a business to run, and the World Series win was just a stepping stone to bigger and brighter dreams.[19]

Fred A. Busse, Mayor of Chicago, and Charles Comiskey (center) at South Side Park for the infamous World Championship Pennant festivities; May 14, 1907; by the Chicago Daily News, Inc. photographer. Chicago History Museum, #SDN-052640.

*   *   *   *

One of Comiskey's dreams was to internationalize baseball, a plan he was working on with old pal Ted Sullivan. To test the waters, he decided that the 1907 team board a train for Mexico for spring training. On March 5, 1907, the team took a five-day train ride to Mexico City. After a few days of resting some, and drinking a lot, the team held their first international intra-squad scrimmage game. For the gawking Mexicans, it seemed like a confusing sport, and judging from the puzzled look on their faces, baseball didn't seem to have the appeal Comiskey expected. Plus, the team complained that they should be playing in the States in front of more supportive fans, but, in actuality, they objected to the trip because they were still angered at the meager bonuses they received after the series title. To offset their complaints, Comiskey let the team finish spring training in El Paso, Texas, and threw in an extra $15,000 to make them happy—he called it an "advance" on their 1907 salaries. Possibly out of a new-found reverence for "The Old Roman," the 1907 Sox season took off strong out of the starting gate.[20]

After a promising 4-1 start, on a cloudy May 14 day, Comiskey organized a 1906 World Series pennant raising ceremony to commence before the game. The event looked promising. It began with a parade, starting from downtown and ending up on the South Side Park field. Riding along with the 1906 team was Comiskey, Ban Johnson, Mayor Fred Busse, First Fire Marshal Jim Horan, the police commissioner, and numerous other politicians and business leaders.

As the procession entered South Side Park, the bands in stadium played, and more than 15,000 fans rose from their seats. The first local personality they recognized was the mayor. Only few cheers went his way, but when they saw Comiskey behind him, the fans let out a huge roar. Next, the parade members exited their automobiles and formed a semi-circle around the heavy pine flagpole. Mayor Busse presented Comiskey with the World Series pennant to be hoisted next to the other pennant flags. For reasons unknown, as Big Jim Horan and the other extinguished guests watched the raising of the pennant, the pole swayed, trembled, let out a pop-crack, and then snapped in two. The crowd's cheers turned to gasps as the shard pole narrowly missed the onlookers and buried into the earth with an enormous thud.[21]

Shadows of Chicago

Quickly, Comiskey scrambled to find a way to raise the flag. Saving his friend some embarrassment, Big Jim Horan stepped forward and suggested that they use a hook-and-ladder truck to raise the new World Series flag. Just as the two were about to put their plan into effect, rain started falling and many people looked for cover. Comiskey decided to forgo the pennant ceremony for another day so he could get the game underway. When the rain looked like it was about to let up, he ordered the team to "play ball." After Mayor Busse threw out the first pitch, it started to pour hard this time and only half the fans could find shelter, resulting in a postponement.[22]

Comiskey, being a very superstitious person, felt that the flag ceremony was a bad omen. His premonitions started to ring true. From May 2 through August 6, the Sox remained in first, but when it was time for the pennant, the Sox choked. Then, in 1908, Fielder Jones quit the team, and the "hitless wonders" just faded into the history books, causing sports reporters to begin calling the White Sox the "winless wonders."

Another ominous incident happened on April 25, 1909, when a fire broke out in the first base pavilion of the South Side Park from a cigar butt and threatened to burn down the grandstand. While firefighters were in the midst of knocking down the blaze, one of Comiskey's workers contacted him by telegraph to tell him the horrible news. Once he received the message, he sat back down to the kitchen table and continued eating his wife's dessert. Still stunned, he received another telegraph from another worker that his friend Big Jim Horan notified them that the fire was out and the only damage was an entire section of 50-cent seats. He wanted to pass the message on to Comiskey that the White Sox would be able to play at the field the following day. Comiskey had no reply. It's unknown how Comiskey's odd behavior reached the press, but the *Trib* remarked that the burning of "The Old

Roman's" stadium was reminiscent of Nero and the burning of Rome.[23]

---

[1] Axelson, G.W. *Commy: The Life Story of Charles A. Comiskey.* Chicago: Riley and Lee Company.
[2] *Ibid.*
[3] *Ibid.*; Snyder, John. *White Sox Journal: Year by Year & Day by Day with the Chicago White Sox Since 1901.* Cincinnati, OH: Clerisy Press.
[4] Snyder.
[5] The following game against the Orioles was postponed for President McKinley's funeral. His assassination opened the way for new the president, Theodore Roosevelt.
[6] Axelson.
[7] Snyder.
[8] Axelson.
[9] Snyder.
[10] The only three longer win streaks were the NY Giants (26 in 1916), Cubs (21 in 1935), and A's (20 in 2002). The A's win streak was topic in the movie *Moneyball.*
[11] Snyder.
[12] *Ibid.*
[13] Billy Sullivan had a batting average of just .212 in 16 big league seasons, the second lowest of any player with at least 3,000 at bats. He patented a chest protector in 1909 that injected compressed air into a wind bag in order to absorb the impact of baseballs.
[14] Snyder.
[15] The Cubs .763 winning percentage is still the best ever (Post 1900 era).
[16] Snyder.
[17] *Ibid.*
[18] Lindberg, Richard C. *Total White Sox. The Definitive Enclyclopedia of the Chicago White Sox.* Chicago: Triumph Books.
[19] Axelson.
[20] Snyder.
[21] "Heavens Forbid Pennant Raising," *Chicago Daily Tribune.* May 15, 1907.
[22] *Ibid.*
[23] "Park Scorched: Fire Destroys 50 Cent Seats and Threatens Grand Stand," *Chicago Daily Tribune,* April 26, 1910.

Shadows of Chicago

Chapter 8

BIG JIM'S FIGHT

In 1906 Big Jim was hired as First Fire Marshal, the highest ranking member of the department, at only 47 years old.[1] His new position required that he work the day's shift from a modest office at City Hall. On a typical day, he'd sit in his office dressed in office clothes, but always kept his shoes unlaced, so he could easily flip them off to put on his "bunkies" (turn-out gear) right next to him if he got a run. If he was summoned to a fire, he'd slap on his bunkies in 54 seconds (one reporter's estimate), jump atop the horse buggy for the downtown runs, or ride along in the automobile if he had to reach the furthest ends of the city. When he wasn't in his office, he kept ready at his home with an alarm ready to ring if he's called out. Needless to say, he rarely ever slept.

He always kept the door to his office open to entertain the constant influx of visitors. He was always willing to let in Mayor Busse or other politicians, or any civilian who wanted to come in to talk. In a *Chicago Daily Tribune* article, one writer described Big Jim in his City Hall office. He commented, "The office chair whirls backward, and with his nimble fingers the laces of his shoes loosened, the shoes flung aside, and in a moment the quiet man at the desk has become a giant, erect in a pair of great hip boots and striding back and forth through the suite of rooms awaiting the '2-11' or the '4-11' alarm that may follow the sounding of the box number. There is a tension in the man, but it is never wearing in its effect. Desk work is gone out of his head; he is the fire fighter until the fire strikes 'out' or until the call comes for the dash in buggy or automobile, according to the distance. From 8:30 in the

Shadows of Chicago

morning until 5 in the afternoon he is at headquarters. One day a week, usually Sunday, he is off duty. His home is merely an annex to headquarters when a serious fire happens."[2]

Reporters enjoyed coming to his office to ask questions, since he was one of the most widely-known personalities in the city, even becoming more popular than Fred Busse. Big Jim's popularity would always upstage Busse's popularity, but the two would always remain close friends.

The ones he had to be careful not to leave behind were city council members, fire department heads, and big businessmen. To keep the friendships alive and not let his newfound status upset jealous associates, he invited them to join him at White Sox games. With the help of his friend Charles Comiskey, he reserved a special section in the stands to entertain some of the wealthiest, most famous personalities in the city.

He also had some of his wealthy acquaintances accompany him on fire runs. A group of riders, also known as "fire fans," began meeting at Big Jim's office at City Hall, excited to be a part of the action they read about in the papers. As soon as the fire fans got word of an extra-alarm blaze, they'd ride along in Big Jim's buggy or race behind him in their autos or on their own horses, sometimes dressed in tailored suits and shiny leather shoes. Often dressed inappropriately for fire call, a few would help firemen lug hoses, remove burning debris, or rescue civilians. Some firefighters appreciated the fans' help at fires and had fun teasing their aristocratic manner and appearance. Some even liked the extra company. But the more the fire fans started showing up to every major fire and loitering around the firehouses, the more the firemen felt they were getting in the way of their duty. Some distrusted them, feeling they represented the same socioeconomic group that typically neglected to give funds for improving the fire department.

Big Jim saw it another way, believing that the more the affluent people were exposed to the dangers firemen faced firsthand, the more they'd be willing to increase funds for improvement. As a matter of fact, Big Jim was right. Money poured into the fire department at a rate never seen before. In just his first year as First Fire Marshal, he gathered enough funds for nine new engine companies, two hook-and-ladder companies, 25 revamped firehouses, 225 new horses, and two high-powered fire boats. Furthermore, he used some of the money to make all of the fire apparatus parts interchangeable so all the fittings, wheels, and axles were uniform—this allowed the fire department to buy parts from the same manufactures in bulk, saving thousands of additional dollars.[3]

Right away he used the additional money to increase firemen's safety and well-being. He immediately increased salaries by 10 percent, and saw to it they had a 24 consecutive hours off every sixth 12 hour working day. In addition, he improved their sleeping quarters, providing comfortable iron beds with springs and hair mattresses.[4] But to keep the firemen from getting too comfortable during downtime, he introduced handball and organized baseball tournaments to improve the quickness and coordination needed during rescues.[5]

His concern for the firefighters' well-being made the men feel like he was one of the guys. Many were relieved that they could call their new First Fire Marshal "Big Jim," rather than the usual big department titles, "chief" or "sir." More importantly, firefighters were happy they had one of their own running the department, not some politician's puppet, but someone who really watched over them—many at the time agreed there was a feeling of pride in the department like never before.

Shadows of Chicago

Partially due to the newfound confidence or to the new budget increase, push-out time improved citywide, and even though the population continued to increase, the total loss from fires from 1906 to 1909 dropped by more than a million dollars.[6] More importantly, civilian and firefighter deaths dropped exponentially. These facts were not enough for Big Jim to be content, because modern industrialization had created conditions that were ripe for another Great Chicago Fire.[7]

* * * *

On August 3, 1908, fire broke out in a freight house at Burlington Railway at 16th and Canal, near the south branch of the Chicago River. That summer's day the city was in the midst of record dry weather and there was a continuous, strong southwest wind, almost identical to the conditions of The Great Chicago Fire. The biggest difference with this fire was that there was a tremendous amount of hazardous materials involved, causing the fire to burn hotter and more inconsistently than any firefighter had ever experienced, including Big Jim.

Supposedly the fire ignited in a grain elevator by someone throwing a lit cigarette among soda potash, saltpeter, and nitroglycerine. This caused such an explosive chemical reaction that caused the 700,000 bushels of wheat and 100,000 bushels of corn stored in the freight house to immediately incinerate. Soon after, several explosions thundered, causing the entire freight house to be blanketed with flames.

Due to the strong southwest wind, flames catapulted to adjoining buildings and sent red-hot cinders to cause additional blazes a half-mile away. Due to hazardous chemicals stored in the buildings, the fires burned so hot that railroad cars and other smaller buildings nearby were cremated in seconds. The biggest threat was that the monstrous fire would jump over the river to the Standard Oil refineries. Detonation of this source would incite a city-wide catastrophe.

The first available firefighters were dumbfounded at the ever-increasing conflagration. Their initial progress was hampered because the closest water source to the scene was a half-mile away, which would require stretching miles of hose. On top of that, temporary plank roadways were needed on top of the railroad tracks, so the horse-drawn five-ton engines could move into position. Once the firefighters moved into position, they were met with breathtaking heat, so hot, in fact, entire companies were forced to drop to their stomachs and crawl "snake-like" so they could continue to guide their hoses towards the fire, while their fellow firefighters kept their hoses on them to keep them from succumbing to the heat. Nearest the heart of the fire, about 40 engine companies were fighting a never-ending battle, and 10 of the horses dropped from the heat.

Big Jim stood with another 24 engines on the north part of the river as a defensive measure to keep the fire from lapping across to the river to the more highly prone structures, and he worked to slow down the fire that had invaded the Loop district. Even though each engine company worked to their fullest potential, it was still not enough against the prevailing southwest winds. So, Big Jim called on the city's three fireboats—each boat had the power of 12 engines. With the roar of the mighty engines, they guzzled water from the river and poured thousands of tons of water on the elevators to prevent the flames from spreading. As one of the boats, the Illinois, directed its heavy streams in the direction of the grain elevators, an explosion caused by the built up gas from the heated grain pushed the wall outward and it crashed onto the boat's bow. Luckily, the ropes of the Illinois were tied to the dock to give firefighters a minute to escape to safety before it plunged 20 feet to the bottom.

Shadows of Chicago

The two remaining boats' aggressive stance against the mighty fire was still not enough against the southwest wind. Numerous explosions continued to shoot flames as far as 200 feet, sending cinders for a ride on the fast-moving wind, igniting roofs and awnings as far east as Wabash and Michigan avenues, leaving fire engine companies to work miles from the initial fire. Several miles northeast the First Ward's battalion had nearly 150 fires raging at once.

After two and a half hours of agonizing firefighting, the exposure fires were knocked and under control, and the boats were used to wash residual fire chemical-soaked grain elevators until the next day.

The day after the fire on August 4th, Big Jim held an urgent press conference. His address began, "For more than two hours I was in dread of a conflagration that would sweep over the city." As he struggled to get the words out he continued, "If the flames had got to the south we would have had a Great Chicago Fire... Still, the department someday may be overmatched unless it is strengthened by the installation of a high pressure water system which is needed as a protection against the peril of great conflagrations. It was certainly a miracle that no one was killed or injured. It was the hottest fire and the hardest to fight I have seen in years... Those business men who, looking from their office windows in the loop district yesterday, thought they saw the flames advancing upon them, must earnestly strive to serve their own interests and the interests of the city by working for the high-pressure system which is needed as a protection."[8]

His address went on to say that the grain elevator fire was proof that a special bureau must be provided to regulate explosives and inflammable matter, and again stressed the need for a high-pressure system in the most congested district of the city and the stockyard district. He also added that the amount of engine companies would need to double, making one for every square mile. He concluded his address with a warning to the public that if city officials don't heed his warnings, there will be insurmountable losses.

* * * *

With the help of his good friend Mayor Busse and his pressure on city council, it became one of the largest fire departments in the world, with 108 engine companies, and 31 hook and ladder companies. From the department's sudden growth, Chicago was a model for other cities' fire departments.

Other city departments took notice of the improvements in fire suppression. On his off days, Big Jim would sometimes travel to other cities around the country to act as a consultant or to take control of major incidents. His most unique assignment occurred on Monday, November 15, 1909, at the Cherry Mine in Cherry, Illinois, 100 miles southwest of Chicago.

He got word that 391 miners were trapped when a hay cart caught fire from a kerosene torch in the mine. Deep within the belly of the mine, fires spread quickly through narrow tunnels, killing many instantly from the flames and smoke; others were trapped, hiding in the furthest recesses of the mine, searching for the ever-depleting fresh air pockets. Not knowing where the men lay trapped, 11 rescuers were blindly lowered into the mine by the main hoisting elevator. When the elevator was raised from the shaft, only the rescuers' charred corpses remained. After seeing this, local firemen, miners, and the rest of the town realized just how helpless the rescue effort was.[9]

Not knowing where to turn, they telegraphed First Fire Marshal Horan in his office. Their urgent plea immediately provoked Big Jim to work out a plan, even though he knew nothing about rescuing the trapped miners.

Shadows of Chicago

He said, "I am going there myself in the morning but the fight will begin before I arrive, so I sent enough men to handle the equipment."

He hand-picked 10 of the best firemen he could find to accompany him on the freight train to Cherry, Illinois. Seeing that he and his men should be well-prepared, he ordered the train stocked with the most powerful fire engine, 5,000 feet of 2 ½ inch hose, 500 feet of 3-inch pipe, 36 extinguishers, 50,000 gallons of water, and, most disturbingly, 300 pine coffins in case the situation was worse than he imagined.[10]

Moments after the supplies were loaded, Big Jim and his men were speeding along the nearly-frozen, flat prairie, listening to the constant clickety-clack of rails and the phuff-phuff of light smoke puffing from the steam locomotive. All the while, they attempted to fathom the problems they would soon face. But before they could consider fire tactics, they arrived at the town's station in record-breaking time, covering about a 100 miles in a little over an hour.[11]

Big Jim and the firemen arrived at the Cherry Mine late Tuesday afternoon to gray skies and high winds and found themselves surrounded by people, pleading for them to save their loved ones. Moving through the tormented crowd, the mine owners, Earling and Taylor, ran up to Big Jim and placed him in control of the rescue and told them about a new dilemma they now faced. They informed them they closed all the hoisting shafts to keep oxygen from fueling the fire, a controversial decision because some of the trapped miners needed outside air to survive. This caused some of the panicked crowd to try to reopen the shafts themselves. Big Jim agreed with the tough decision the mine owners made, because he also believed a few miners may have to suffocate so that others would not be burned alive.

Matthew Drew

The first thing he did was slightly open the two shafts—one to allow for enough space for the fire engine's four-inch hose to send water down the shaft and the other to place a fan to suck out the smoke. All the while, he knew that some of the miners hidden in the narrow tunnels might drown from the incoming water, but he found it more important to decrease the mine temperature before beginning rescue operations. The temperature was near 115 degrees, and that wasn't near the core of the fire. To decrease the temperature, he had the fire engine pump a 100 gallons per minute—which may sound like a lot, but the engines were capable of up to 500 gallons a minute. Any more water may have collapsed the fragile wooden beams keeping the mine in place.

At the end of a long and grueling first day, Big Jim decided it was too dangerous for the rescue effort to begin. He said, "The shaft will not be unsealed until I am assured that the fire in the mine is practically extinguished... As I stated before, no man can enter the mine and live today. The company is not anxious to sacrifice more human lives in the mine." He knew his men were anxious, though; so he told them secretly they would soon get a chance to come face-to-face with the fire.

Late Wednesday night, he found an opportunity to launch the first offensive against the fire. With the help of a few volunteers, Big Jim, a few of his men, and 300 feet of hose were lowered dozens of feet by the hoisting shaft. Once they lowered to the densest smoke, felt the rising heat, and saw the bodies of dead miners, they knew they had the best entryway toward the fire. The tunnel was pitch-dark because the lights lining the sides of the tunnels provided little illumination, due to the heavy black smoke which had little place to ventilate out. On the other hand, Big Jim and his men knew by experience that the dark, smoky conditions meant they were advancing toward the fire.

Shadows of Chicago

Seeing the first signs of progress being made, he ordered more mine shafts opened to dissipate the heavy smoke—even though this would allow the fires to rekindle again from the fresh oxygen. The firemen didn't mind. It was a relief for them to finally see what they were fighting instead of shooting their hoses blindly into the pitch-darkness. At first the fight seemed like any other structure fire they experienced in Chicago. They moved the hoses through the network of tunnels and make-shift rooms, extinguishing the burning wood fuel. But after a while, they found new pitfalls they weren't used to encountering. The further they advanced the lines to the deeper parts of the mine the more they had to avoid rocks from dropping down upon them or cutting off their means of egress. Not only that, but the fragile wooden skeleton snapped above them, while mule carcasses and mine carts had to be hauled from pathways.[12]

Big Jim was aware of the stress this was causing his men, so he had them work in shifts of five at a time. Time and time again the firefighters took turns battling the blaze, often surfacing for fresh air or to gather more hose to reach every possible tunnel they could. When the most weakened men returned from battle, doctors and nurses attended to them. Others refused to rest until they could find live bodies.[13]

On Friday, after four sleepless days of intense fighting, 27 live miners were found by the Chicago firemen and the volunteers. The miners were huddled together, barely breathing in one of the deep nooks of the mine. Another 291 miners weren't so lucky.

After this greatest mine disaster in U.S. history, Big Jim's response to the incident became a textbook method of containing fires in mines and rescuing trapped miners.

*   *   *   *

Matthew Drew

In 1910, it concerned Big Jim that the fire department was about to respond to more than 9,000 fires—the most ever before in one year.[14] Therefore, he believed that new methods had to be taken to counteract the ever-expanding growth in fires, so he established the Bureau of Combustibles, the forerunner of the present day Fire Prevention Bureau. Also, his plan to increase the amount of motorized equipment to cover every square mile of the city was about to pass the city council's approval. As always, he lobbied unsuccessfully for a high-pressure water system in the downtown business district and the Union Stockyards.

Finding the funds for a high-pressure system in the Stockyards would be his biggest priority and toughest obstacle. Philip Danforth Armour, Gustavus Swift, and Nelson Morris, "The Big Three Meat Barons," as they were commonly called, had Big Jim's political clout in their pocket. This included even his closest friend in office, Mayor Busse. On one occasion when Big Jim confronted Busse about the high-pressure system, he responded, "We are ready to take the matter up and do something."[15]

Busse never was never able to do something about the high-pressure system, possibly because he could not risk losing the support of the wealthiest people in the city, and plus, he was already losing powerful friends as he handled the issues in the city's vice district.

Any time a city official requested assistance from The Big Three for the multi-million-dollar high-pressure system in the stockyards, they would not outright refuse the request. They'd just walk away. They had this kind of power because the meat packers controlled the city, since they also controlled most of the money coming into the city. This never-ending struggle would continue up to the last day of Big Jim's life.

Shadows of Chicago

---

[1] The highest ranking Chicago department head is now known as the Fire Commissioner.

[2] "Jim Horan Answers the Call," *Chicago Tribune*. April 14 1907.

[3] Rice, John. *Research Data, 1910 Stockyards Fire,* November 28, 2001.

[4] Kolomay, Marion. *Account of the Great Stockyard Fire.*

[5] The handball played in Chicago and other American cities at the time was believed to derive from Irish Gaelic handball that was played since the 15th Century. It was mostly played in a 40x20 four-walled court. Players used their hands to smack a small "black ball"—that bounced wildly—and was painful when it struck the body. Most handball courts in today's firehouses are used primarily for racquetball—a somewhat less physically demanding sport. Down-time is a term for the space between calls. It varies from company-to-company, day-to-day, and run-to-run.

[6] "Push-out time" refers to the time it takes for fire apparatuses to leave the station. The total loss from fires in Chicago dropped from 4,179,235 in 1906 to 3,046,797 in 1909.

[7] "James Horan Address," *Chicago Daily Tribune,* August 23, 1908.

[8] *Ibid.*

[9] Tintori, Karen. *Trapped: The 1909 Cherry Mine Disaster*. New York: Atria Books, 2002.

[10] *Ibid.*

[11] "Chicago Water to Mine Fire," *Chicago Daily Tribune,* Nov 16, 1909.

[12] Tintori.

[13] "Chicago Water to Mine Fire," *Chicago Daily Tribune,* Nov 16, 1909.

[14] In 1910, the total number of alarms exceeded 12,000; actual fires were 9,083.

[15] "Ready for High Pressure: Mayor Calls Conference On New Water System." *Chicago Daily Tribune.* May 18, 1907.

Chapter 9

HIGH PRESSURE ON BUSSE

In 1907, at the start of his four-year term, Mayor Busse was suffering from stress caused by pressure from citizens demanding that he do something about the city's gambling, liquor, and prostitution issues. The ever-growing tension made him look well beyond his current age of 41—he had only a little hair left on the back of his head and temples, permanent black bags under his eyes, and he was now the heaviest he ever had been. This was due, for the most part, because every day in the papers and in person, people criticized him for his inactivity at the ever-growing social problems, as well as reporters increasingly delving into his personal affairs. One time when reporters questioned him about closing down liquor establishments, he blurted out, "They don't need anyone sleuthing around after me. They can always get me any evening at J.C. Murphy's saloon, Clark Street and North Avenue." Obviously, he didn't attend his favorite saloon for its ambiance. Instead, he was busy getting drunk, the very sin his critics sought to rid the city of.

    It is also ironic that the public hounded him for not closing down houses of prostitution, when, as history proves, he spent many years hanging out at whorehouses in the Levee, and using his pull to keep the law from affecting their businesses. Prior to the mayoral election of 1907, one of famous madams of the Levee, Vic Shaw, printed his face on coupons to lure customers inside. The coupon declared this prior to his Busse's election:

OUR PAL
IF HE WINS AND YOU

Shadows of Chicago

> FIND THIS CARD IN THE PARLOR BRING
> IT TO MADDAM
> YOU GET $5.00 IN TRADE
> FREE
> ELECTION NIGHT
> ONLY[1]

Once Busse became mayor, he no longer wanted his face associated with the whorehouses, but it seemed he could never escape his past. For example, *The Chicago Daily Socialist* told the horrific story of an Irish girl and her subjection into white slavery at the Everleigh Club, and how Mayor Fred Busse, a regular at the club, kept "the arm of the law off this white slave gang."[2] There's no doubt that the "white slave gang" would continue to need the mayor, politicians, and police to protect their establishments.

And the fact was that Busse needed the votes coming in from the vice districts for his 1907 mayoral election and would continue to need them if he wanted to be reelected in 1911. If he went on a crusade to close the vice districts, he would enrage both Republican and Democratic politicians—both party members made a boatload of money from the debauchery in the Levee, particularly first ward Aldermen Hinky-Dink Kenna and Bathhouse Coughlin. Not to mention all the flak he'd catch from underworld bosses like "Big Jim" Colosimo. So, as his mayoral term proceeded, he had to tread lightly as he sought to improve his public persona.

Busse thought it would be to his advantage to at least humor the righteous people that continually pestered him at his office at City Hall. The biggest thorn in his side was Arthur Burrage Farwell, president of the Chicago Law and Order League. On three separate occasions in 1907, Farwell, with dozens of league's supporters, approached Busse in his office, demanding that he enforce anti-white slave laws in the Levee. On the third occasion, they told

Busse to get rid of the First Ward Ball, after witnessing the most notorious, devilish orgy in person. Farwell said, "A real description of the 1907 ball is simply unprintable. You must stop them from putting another on this year. You must stop this disgrace to Chicago. You must stop it in the name of the young men who will be ruined there." Mayor Busse responded sullenly, "What do you want me to do, gentlemen?" Farwell pressed on: "You can refuse a liquor license. That will stop them. Mr. Busse, you cannot in good conscience issue a liquor license for this affair. Suppose you had a friend whose character and life you prized highly. How would you like to have such scenes of debauchery as allowed at this ball to bring degradation and perhaps destruction to your friend? Prevent a reputation of this vile orgy!" Busse sat silently for a moment, careful how to approach his biggest critics, and then he said a liquor license was already issued for the year's ball. In an effort to not anger Farwell further, he said, "I want to find out myself how this is."3

After a few weeks, to pacify Farwell and his supporters, and possibly to improve his image, Farwell and he set out with a group to view the Levee—even though this was probably just a trip down memory lane for him. Reluctantly, members of the league, fellow advisors, and he walked down the Levee's cobblestoned streets, viewing houses of ill-refute and X-rated plays, like "Moonshiner's Daughter." After their visit, Busse held a press conference on January 2, 1907, and announced that heavy fines were handed out and many of the shows are taken away from the Levee. Moreover, Busse announced that he was going to appoint a vice commission to look at Chicago's gambling, liquor, and prostitution problems.4

After Busse made the announcement, he asked Hinky-Dink and Bathhouse to close down the First Ward Ball. Soon after his plea, he told an unnamed reporter that one of the ball's supporters threatened to bomb his house if he didn't stop pressing the issue.5 Possibly out of fear, he called a meeting at his office with one of the Lords of Levee, "Bathhouse" Coughlin, and the city's religious leaders, Arthur Farwell, and the Reverend E. A. Bell, head of the Midnight Mission. In an effort to make as little waves as possible, he tried to have the warring factions come to a peaceful resolution. Not surprisingly, Bathhouse and the two religious leaders had it out and no resolution was ever reached. However, after several days of negotiation (presumably Busse made a deal with Bathhouse and Hinky-Dink), Bathhouse proclaimed that due to negative public opinion he'd "[bow] to the goody-good people of Chicago" and end the First Ward Ball. The following year the infamous duo threw another ball, without the wine and women this time. It turned out to be a bust. Even though the infamous First Ward Ball came to end, Hinky-Dink and Bathhouse concentrated on keeping the vice in the Levee alive.[6]

    In 1908, Busse married Josephine Lee, a black poet, and the daughter of a celebrated artist. Perhaps it was his new wife that softened his hard stance on turning a blind-eye to prostitution, or maybe it was the years of bombarding religious groups that finally got to him. Either way, Busse would make the most prominent move during his political career.

    He appointed the Chicago Vice Commission in 1910. The 30 man committee was set to make a list of every place and every person involved in prostitution, study the conditions of other cities, and come to a conclusion to be presented to city. Busse said during the March 1910 press conference, "A short time ago I received communication from representatives of the federated protestant churches calling my attention to the vice in Chicago, and requesting that a commission be appointed to study the subject, with a view to determining a plan of control as well as considering the moral and physical harm which results from vice." He went on to say that Chicago's problems were the same problems going on in other cities.[7]

Possibly Busse referenced the plight over "other cities" in his press conference, because other cities, like Chicago, allowed segregated vice districts only to keep their red-light affairs away from the general public. And perhaps he thought that if prostitution remained a regulated business within confines of the Levee limits, then residential and business areas would mostly remain free of vice. Hopefully, this would be enough to satisfy the religious do-gooders and, more importantly, allow Levee bosses to still make a buck. This in turn would hopefully solidify his chances for reelection.

With this in mind, Busse could not have fathomed that the introduction of Chicago Vice Commission would have such an impact as it would on the national stage. As news of vile conditions in the Levee and elsewhere came to light, President Howard Taft sent a letter to Congress, bringing about the federal mandate of the White-Slave Traffic Act.[8] The White-Slave Traffic Act, better known as the Mann Act, was passed as a U.S. law on June 25, 1910. The law would prohibit the interstate transport of females for "immoral purposes." The Mann Act states, "That any person who shall knowingly transport... any woman or girl for the purpose of prostitution or debauchery... shall be deemed guilty of a felony, and upon conviction thereof shall be punished by a fine not exceeding five thousand dollars, or by imprisonment of not more than five years, or by both such fine and imprisonment, in the discretion of the court." Even though the Mann Act's primary intent was to stop human trafficking, it would serve as framework for the country's aim to criminalize other forms of immorality. Thus, Chicago became the forefront of the nation's aim to criminalize corruption.

* * * *

Shadows of Chicago

In 1910, almost as a slap in the face to the white slavery commissions, Colosimo's Café opened at 2126 Wabash, smack dab in the heart of the Levee. The impressive décor attracted many of Levee's richest denizens and the city's elite. Judging from the ambiance in the café, and the way Big Jim Colosimo catered to his guests, it would seem that he was abandoning the pleasure industry for more legit business interests. In actuality, the café served as a front for the white slavery ring that he ran from the café's back rooms. While his back-room business kept the heat off his dozens of brothels, other brothels in Levee were raided on a regular basis.

There was no doubt that Levee brothels required the white slavery movement if they wanted their businesses to survive. To remain afloat they needed the constant supply of fresh new girls to their regular customers. Since law enforcement was now cracking down, every brothel required Colosimo's white slavery ring to supply the market. This paved the way for Colosimo to be master pimp of the Levee.

Instead of pimping out the new girls himself, he turned to inside white slave operators like Maurice Van Bever. Colosimo partnered with Bever, and Bever's wife, Julia, to transport several hundred young girls from all over the country. In turn, they sold the girls to madams for $300 a girl.[9] Their arrangement worked out well until Bever was prosecuted and sent to jail, while Colosimo, as always, got away scot-free.

He remained untouchable due to his ongoing friendship with Hinky-Dink and Bathhouse, for they had the top law enforcement in the Levee's 22nd District in their pockets. But even the top cops weren't beyond getting busted. For instance, the 22nd District's Captain Edward McCann was indicted for providing protection to brothel madams. He was sent to jail for "five counts of bribery and five counts of malfeasance as an officer."[10] Soon after, McCann would die due to mysterious reasons.[11]

After McCann's black eye on the police department's image, Mayor Busse was forced by public opinion to fire his prior appointment, Captain George Shippy, because McCann worked under Shippy's not-so-watchful eye. Busse replaced the worthless Shippy with the seemingly non-corruptible Col. Leroy Steward as top cop. In *Sin in the Second City*, Karen Abbot described the new chief: "He spoke of his interest in theosophy and 'primal topics.' Delicate wire-rimmed glasses sat low on his pointed nose, a pipe remained clenched perpetually between his lips. There would be no unseemly talk of graft payments during his tenure."[12] Needless to say, Captain Steward's reign marked a difficult time for the brothel owners.

Despite Captain Steward's and the Attorney General's Office's aggressive pressure on Colosimo, he would continue his white slavery networks, brothels, and gambling dens with little interference. His domain would actually increase well beyond the Levee's streets, helping to establish himself as Chicago's first vice lord. By the end of 1910, his criminal enterprise would help protect the 25,000 women and 10,000 men engaged in the prostitution business.[13]

As a top member of the outfit, his biggest nemesis would not come from the police department or the Attorney General's Office. Rather, pressure came from a group of which he was once a member: The Black Hand.[14]

The Black Hand was a band of Italian criminals that worked mostly in cities like New York and Chicago. Their signature trademark was a rough drawing of a black hand and a threat written in Italian. The intimidating note usually threatened death to anyone who did not comply with their monetary demands.[15]

Colosimo had paid out to Black Hand aggressors before, but he was sick of it. Supposedly, he called on his nephew from New York Johnny "The Fox" Torrio, a boxing promoter, to take care the Black Hand members.

On Nov 22, 1911, police came to a shooting at 2047 Archer Road. Police found two men shot dead on the scene, another one was found crawling, leaving a trail of blood behind him. The two dead were off-the-boat Italian hoodlums, Pasquale Damico and Francisco Denello. Francisco's brother, Stefano Denello, refused to rat to police officers, but wanted to speak to Colosimo before he died. Before he passed, the two talked. About what, nobody knows.[16]

After the shooting, the ever-grateful Colosimo gave his nephew Torrio the Saratoga brothel, two doors down from the Everleigh Club. Soon, he would make him the second most formidable member of the outfit.

---

[1] Abbott, Karen. *Sin in the Second City. Madams, Ministers, Playboys and the Battle for America's Soul.* New York: Random House, 2007.

[2] *Ibid.*

[3] *Ibid.*

[4] "Busse Sees Levee; Changes Ordered," *Chicago Daily Tribune,* January 2, 1907.

[5] Bilek, Arthur J. *The First Vice Lord: Big Jim Colosimo and the Ladies of the Levee.* Nashville: Cumberland House Publishing, 2008.

[6] *Ibid.*

[7] "Mayor Appoints Vice Commission: Thirty Prominent Students of Social Conditions Will Try to Solve Problem." *Chicago Daily Tribune.* March 6, 1910.

[8] Bilek.

[9] *Ibid.*

[10] *Ibid.*

[11] "Pictures McCann As King of the Levee" *Chicago Daily Tribune.* September 10, 1909.

[12] Abbott.

[13] Lehman-Clarkson, F.M. *White Slave Hell, or With Christ at Midnight in the Slums of Chicago.* Chicago: The Christian Witness Company, 1910.

[14] Bilek.

[15] *Ibid.*

[16] *Ibid.*

Chapter 10

FRIDAY AT COMISKEY PARK

Comiskey was horrified when he heard that opening day at Comiskey Park was scheduled for July 1, 1910, a Friday, no less. Upon hearing the news, he asked that Ban Johnson, President of the American League, change the date for new park's opening day festivities. Even though a schedule change wouldn't take much on Johnson's part, he outright refused his former friend's request.[1]

Comiskey, being a firm believer in ancient Irish superstitions, believed Friday was the unluckiest day and, worse, beginning a journey on that day was bound to bring misfortune. Even though his team's "journey" only took them four blocks to the north at 35th and Shields, the move activated the most infamous decade in baseball's history.

Before the 1910 baseball season started, a series of unpromising events plagued the team. On February 28, the Sox team (minus Comiskey) was well on their way to their training camp in San Francisco, when in the early morning, as their train cruised along on top of the Rocky Mountains at more than 10,000 feet near Dotsero, Colorado, the conductor saw an oncoming eastbound train jump the track and plow into the snow. Luckily, the conductor jammed the brakes on the heavy steel wheels, causing the train to screech to a halt, narrowly avoiding plowing into the oncoming train. Everybody was a little shaken up, but no one was hurt seriously. The team was delayed nine hours until the wrecking crew cleared the snow and debris from the track.[2]

When the Sox team arrived in Frisco, they were dead tired and had lost a day at training camp. But just when the team was up and ready to play ball, their star catcher Billy

Shadows of Chicago

Sullivan stepped on a rusty nail. As Sully toughed-out his injury by playing on the field, he ignored his friends' advice to see a doctor; instead, he consulted a nutty pharmacist who prescribed a heavy dose of turpentine to cure the injury. Due to the poor medical advice, he almost lost his leg. But once a more experienced doctor took care of him, he saved the leg, but wouldn't play again until early July.[3]

Another freakish accident happened two months prior to the season opener. As Comiskey, Ban Johnson, and others in baseball management were several miles from their destination at Frankfort, Kentucky, their train collided with another train, causing cars from both trains to uncouple and fall off the track. As a result of the accident, there were 12 serious injuries—none of the injured included Comiskey, Johnson, or members of the Sox organization. This horrific incident was Comiskey's second train accident, and the team members' second in two months.[4]

Weeks after the accident, in an effort to restore good luck to his team, Comiskey held a groundbreaking ceremony at Comiskey Park on St. Patrick's Day. During the event, a "lucky" Irish green brick along with Irish sod was placed in the stadium.[5] Maybe due to the newfound luck, the Sox team came raging out into the 1910 season. They stormed into opening day at Comiskey Park with an impressive 9-1-1 record under their belt.

As scheduled, on Friday July 1, 1910, Comiskey Park opened to eager fans anxious to get away from the decaying wooden bleachers at South Side Park. In contrast, the new stadium was a much larger and constructed of concrete and steel—much more impervious to fire and other unlucky environmental factors that might arise. The look of the new stadium would never have the visual appeal of other stadiums around the country, like Yankee Stadium or Fenway, but to Sox's blue-collar fans, its rough-look suited them just fine. The only complaint was the foul animal odors coming from the Union Stockyards, but when the awful smell blew their way, they knew the wind would also carry the baseballs towards the outfield fences, increasing the chances for an exciting hitting frenzy.

Besides their impressive new ball park, fans were treated to an extravagant pre-game celebration, including a parade that took off from downtown, four military bands, and a visit from local and national VIPs.[6] The total cost of the event, the new stadium, and other essentials, was near $700,000, all raised by Comiskey.[7] The pretty penny he spent seemed to be all worth it. That day he was all smiles as he sat in the grandstand with his closest associates, of the guests were Fred Busse and Big Jim Horan—the game marked the last time Comiskey, Horan, and Busse would all be in the same place together.[8]

The happy day for Comiskey turned into one that fulfilled his superstitious premonitions. The bad omens started to come true by the end of the game in front of 24,000 fans in attendance. The Sox lost 2-0 against the St. Louis Browns, and also lost the team's captain Rollie Zieder due to an injury. More team injuries would soon follow. This would be one of the reasons the team had an 11-game losing slump between July 8 and 21, a new record in the books for the Sox team that had already suffered from "hitless" disease. The hitless streak would continue, landing the team in sixth place and finally netting a batting average of .211, the worst of any team in the 20th Century.[9]

Comiskey could not have known that the team's darkest shadow would come in the form of a player. Before the 1910 season Comiskey picked up a rough character from the minors, first basemen Arnold "Chick" Gandil. Gandil was 6'2" and had a permanent scowl on his face, a warning to everyone to stay out of his way. He was a high school dropout from Oakland, California, who ran away from home to the Arizona desert to play ball and work part-time as a boilermaker in the copper mines. When his team moved to Mexico, he followed, and also began training as a heavyweight fighter.

Due to poor performance and prevailing nasty attitude, at the end of the 1910 season, Comiskey sent Gandil back down to the minors.[10] However, the dark shadow would reemerge with the Sox during the World Champion season of 1917.

---

[1] Lindberg, Richard C. *Total White Sox. The Definitive Encyclopedia of the Chicago White Sox.* Chicago: Triumph Books.

[2] Sanborn, I.E., "Sox Held For Nine Hours in Train Wreak" *Chicago Daily Tribune*, March 1, 1910.

[3] Snyder, John. *White Sox Journal: Year by Year & Day by Day with the Chicago White Sox Since 1901.* Cincinnati, OH: Clerisy Press.

[4] Lindberg.

[5] Snyder.

[6] Sanborn, I. E., "Commy to Greet Sox Fans Today," *Chicago Daily Tribune*, July 10 1910.

[7] Snyder.

[8] Sanborn, I. E., "Commy to Greet Sox Fans Today," *Chicago Daily Tribune*, July 10 1910.

[9] Lindberg.

[10] Snyder.

Chapter 11

THE WATCHDOGS AND THE YARDS

In 1910, Chicago's population rose to just about 2.2 million, a 1.6 million increase in 20 years.[1] Possibly no other metropolitan area had grown so fast—and just like an overgrown puppy, the city was young, awkward, and needed to sprawl out.

The Chicago Union Stockyards provided plenty of jobs for the bursting population to fill refrigerated railroad cars and ships going to the most remote areas of the United States as well as four continents. All over the world their bright yellow freighters boasted a message: "We Feed the World" and "The Hog Butcher of the World" in large, painted letters. For many Chicagoans, the Union Stockyards represented a way to endure the future. For others, it was a place of unimaginable horror. Within the yards, as well as the budding metropolis, great industrial advancements were causing even more dangers.

As the industry sprang up during the middle of the nineteenth century, the natural landscape in around Chicago changed as well. For a long time the wet, marshy prairie land remained unmoved by the first white settlers, so at first the tall prairie grass, wild rye, eight-foot hemp, six-foot blue stems, and other plant species and wild animals continued to flourish in the marshy land.[2]

But as the population increased towards the end of the nineteenth century, settlers and domesticated animals trampled the once-flourishing wild grass prairies. Once the wild prairies became fenced in and the wet marshes drained, short grass prairies sprouted, providing an ideal

Shadows of Chicago

farming land—and to the more opportunistic farmer, a rangeland for domesticated grazing animals.

Across the rangelands southwest of Chicago, cowboys drove cattle to small slaughterhouses in the heavier populated areas. The problem was that as the cowboys drove cattle across the prairies the animals lost weight, so to keep the cattle fat and to allow pigs and sheep to make the long march to the buyers, the railway was introduced. Within only a few decades of the first settlements railroad tracks cobwebbed around the Midwest merging into Chicago, scarring the natural landscape forever. And so, the success of the railroads marked the end of the area's wild, natural terrain.[3]

As the amount of railroad companies grew and fought for new business, each company sought to have a vested interest in stockyards throughout the country. As a result, several railroad companies fronted 90 percent of the money to build the Chicago Union Stockyards on Christmas Day 1865.[4]

The yards were built, like many early settlements, on the swampy prairies of the Southwest Side, five miles from the city's center. It became so large and efficient that the smaller slaughterhouses could no longer compete with their prices, so after a few decades Chicago packers dominated more than three quarters of the American meat supply.

By 1910, most of the 93 million people in the nation and those living in several other countries found that the yards were the cheapest and easiest way to get their meat products. As a result, it was the world's most impressive slaughterhouse and industrial complex in the world, slaughtering close to five million hogs, two million cattle, and three million sheep a year, while the daily slaughtering averaged about 25,000 cattle, 50,000 hogs and 25,000 sheep.[5] The Union Stockyards was more profitable than most cities in the nation at the time, having its own restaurants, banks, hotels, and water reservoirs.[6]

Matthew Drew

The thousands of packers and people from the surrounding neighborhoods spent so much time at the yards they nicknamed the area Packers' Town—common slang united the words together to form "Packingtown."[7] The ironic difference between Packingtown and the other industrialized cities was that the people walked amongst the thousands of animals waiting to be slaughtered.

The yards must have seemed like a dream job for new employees, since they worked in greatest packing facility in the country. This fact led most to believe there was a chance they could one day own a home and, maybe, if they're fortunate, advance to a higher position. Most, however, would be dismayed to find that their new job involved more horrors than promises.

On the level of hierarchy, new yard workers ranked just above the animals in the pens. All in all, owners cared more about the money the meat production generated than the workers who were employed there. The most infamous owners, Swift, Morris, and Armour, known in political circles as "The Big Three Meat Barons" were ready to risk everything, including their employees, to remain on top of the nation's food chain. Their monopoly capitalized the meat market and controlled politicians, including Mayor Fred Busse, who bowed to their every whim, allowing them to avoid paying some municipal taxes.[8] But to remain the most dominant meat packing industry nationwide, they had to imagine new marketing and administrative strategies.

It was decided that the best way to increase production was by using the by-products of the entire animal. The new packer's catchphrase became, "We use every part of the hog but the squeal."[9] For example, blood was collected from the floor to make fertilizer; the intestines were used to make violin strings and sausage casings; hooves, horns, and muscle were used for glue; and hair was used to make combs and toothbrushes. Other meat refuse (usually handled by the female workforce), known as "deviled ham," was put in the low market for those unable to afford prime cuts—sometimes sawdust, animal droppings, dirt, or workers' missing appendages ended up in those meat by-products.

On the slaughtering floor of Packingtown, otherwise known as the "lightning line," workers splashed in inch-deep bloody mud up to 12 hours a day, risking injury and diseases. Most occurred during the cold winters. Because the lightning line was unheated, workers would often tie their feet in old newspapers or dip their feet in the hot carcasses for warmth. The same could not be done with the hands and gloves because they got in the way of meat cutting dexterity, so there was no way to warm their hands. On many occasions fingers would grow so numb that they could not feel a deep cut or even notice when the knife slipped and cut off their own fingers.[10]

Conversely, during the summers, the 100-degree heat on the floor made the 12 hour workdays a living hell. If workers dropped due to heat exhaustion, if a hand was lost, or if they developed rheumatism from tainted blood, they would be most likely be fired on the spot. Members of the lightning line had to hide injuries or stronger-looking workers were called from outside the gates the next day to take their place.

Each worker on the lightning line had his or her own duty to kill, gut, and cut up hundreds of animals per hour at inhuman speeds. Within 10 minutes, a perfectly healthy animal became a lifeless piece of meat in the cooling locker. The most gruesome job belonged to the men on the hog disassembly line. As hogs screamed, squealed, bit and kicked workers, their legs were chained to an enormous wheel. First, the "sticker" cut the throat of the hog, severing main arteries, bathing him in blood. Second, the "splitters" then cut the hog in half. And third, as the hog was still twitching, the "headman" decapitated it in two or three direct cuts. The killing process for cattle was a little less grisly. One man would hit the cattle square on the forehead with a sledgehammer, leaving the animal unconscious or dead before it was pulled onto the killing bed to be slaughtered.[11]

Once the hogs and the cattle were drained of all life and blood, they were dissected by the "deboner," who removed the bones with the least possible damage to meat cuts. One worker said, "Each man [was] working as if a demon were after him." The work on the lightning line became even less human the more mechanized it became.[12]

Modeled after Ford's auto assembly line, the disassembly line replaced many of the workers with tools and machinery—the defective equipment became a greater concern for the workers.[13] The workers at the end of day, covered from head-to-toe in dry blood and sweat, marched out of Packingtown beaten and dead-tired—looking like the wounded animals did, just before being slaughtered.

The general public was first introduced to the horrors of Packingtown from novelist Upton Sinclair in *The Jungle*, published in 1906. He said, "One could not stand and watch long without becoming philosophical, without beginning to deal in symbols and similes, and to hear the hog-squeal of the universe." *The Jungle* alerted the public to workers' rights, safety, and sanitation issues in the workplace. The Food and Drug Act was passed soon after to improve conditions in slaughterhouses throughout the nation. But even though the public became aware of the horrors of Packingtown and several laws were enacted, the people still had to work, refrigerator cars needed to roll, butchers cabinets waited to be filled, and families throughout the nation wanted meat on their plates. The fact remained: Packingtown kept Chicago at the forefront of industrialism, so it dictated all the rules.

In 1910, The Big Three Meat Barons decided that the best way to keep their rich bellies full was to hire more immigrants who were willing to accept the low wages. The

Shadows of Chicago

Big Three paid workers only $23 million in wages for $325 million of product.[14] Two-thirds of the male workforce of Packingtown was making an average of 15 cents an hour, and an average weekly wage $9.50—at a time the average cost to feed a family of five was $15.

Regardless of the low pay, like the livestock traveling in from the west, immigrants came to Chicago by the trainloads daily, occupying two-thirds of the yard's workforce. The Big Three knew that the greater the influx of fresh immigrants, the harder it was for workers to organize and strike because barriers between different ethnic groups made organization less successful. As a result, a lot of money was saved separating workers into ethnic and skill divisions. So, it was cheaper for owners to replace skilled Irish and German butchers with unskilled Lithuanians, Slavs, Poles, Ukrainians, Russians, and Jews.[15]

The Irish and German butchers and their families that used to crowd the streets together outside the yards had moved blocks away in separate ethnic neighborhoods. Many of the low-paid Irish packed into the already crowded Canaryville neighborhood, to the east and south of Packingtown.[16] Canaryville already had a reputation for its rowdy, hard-drinking Irishmen and as being one of the toughest neighborhoods in the city.[17] Not surprisingly, throughout the neighborhood many Irish would resent the unskilled Eastern Europeans that replaced their Packingtown jobs. Irish gangs decided to terrorize their less politically-savvy neighbors, hustling them out of their small paychecks. As Eastern Europeans struggled to learn English, they were overrun by those who spoke the language. As a result, many sought solace with those with common languages or backgrounds.

The Eastern Europeans, mostly Lithuanians, crowded into the "Back of the Yards" neighborhood, situated south and west of Packingtown. The new immigrants had no idea they walked into a bottomless pit.

Low wages from the stockyards and the constant influx of poor immigrants turned the Back of the Yards into the nation's worst slum. What had once been a small town-like neighborhood suddenly became choked with 35,000 more immigrant families who occupied tenements and small double-decker frame houses.[18]

The most congested area in the Back of the Yards was between 40th and 42nd streets on Ashland Avenue, otherwise known as "Whiskey Row," named from the hundreds of saloons lining a distance of only a block and a half. Many saloon keepers would also act as slumlords, cramming an average of 16 men and women into boarding rooms, and they'd be lucky to get a single mattress to sleep on. If the slum tenants needed to eat, they'd walk down to the saloon for free food—but only if they bought drinks first.[19] Most of the saloons' floors were sprinkled with sawdust to hide the vomit, booze, and dried blood and soot from the yards.[20]

Drunken fistfights and robberies were more common on Whiskey Row than any other place in the city, even greater than the Levee. During the day and throughout the night, paddy-wagons would run up and down the hardened mud street that divided the saloons to haul away the bloodied fighters and thieves.

Whiskey Row was an easy place for the poor immigrants to spend their meager paychecks. Some were lonely and needed companionship; others needed entertainment to forget about their hellish job at Packingtown; but most probably found the vile saloons a welcome relief from their smelly neighborhood.

The most persistent stench imaginable surrounded the residents of the Back of the Yards neighborhood. From the east came the smell of the smokestacks that belched burned flesh from Packingtown's killing floor, as well as livestock manure from the pens. From the west came the smell of the city's largest garbage dump. Just north of the neighborhood was "Bubbly Creek"—sometimes creating a toxic scum so thick small animals were seen walking across it. Needless to say, the sanitary conditions were the worst in the world.[21]

Decaying matter from the stockyards poisoned the air and spread disease. Tuberculosis, diphtheria, malaria, and typhoid rates were the highest in the country. There were no antibiotics or doctors available, so the sick either improved or they died. The toxic environment from Packingtown not only spread disease in the Back of the Yards, it hit the rest of Chicago as well. In 1910 Chicago's life expectancy was only 47.3 years, with a large number dying from tuberculosis.[22]

In the Back of the Yards the infant death rate raised to five times that of any other part of the city, killing one out of every three infants—most likely due to disease and malnourishment. Due to low wages, families were forced to scavenge food from Packingtown's garbage dumps—or if blessed, they would have enough money to buy a chunk of deviled ham or a fresh vegetable. Large families would eat their minute portions while Armour's "We Feed the World" meat-stacked railcars departed the yards just south of their homes.

A committee of reformers sought to improve living conditions in the Back of the Yards slum, but since the Big Three controlled city government only minor improvements were made. They felt it was better for business that the poor stay poor, so they'd be less likely strike for higher wages. They were right, because it wasn't until decades later that the Packingtown workers were able to organize and strike successfully.[23]

But even though higher wages were on the distant horizon for the Back of the Yards residents, the black smoke from the yards could not completely darken the neighborhood. In 1910 there was hope brewing in the slum that The Big Three Meat Barons didn't expect. People began venturing outside of Packingtown for work; sports such as horse racing and baseball thrived; children clogged the libraries to read or would escape outside to catch frogs and snakes in the drainage ditches; and there were wildflowers that still bloomed in trash-filled prairies.

For most of the people that lived in Packingtown, there was no radio to listen to, many could not read, and no one could afford a ticket to a White Sox game. Therefore, there were no sports heroes or famous personalities to talk about. Many of the stories told were about firemen, especially the ones in their own neighborhood.

* * * *

Outside of Engine 59's firehouse in November 1910, the cold wind from Canada and western prairies would often blow feathery drifts of snow, hiding some of the smell of the livestock manure and oily smoke from the stockyards. The steaming breath of restless livestock hovered above the pens separated by the wooden alleyways. Even on the colder days in November the firemen could hear the "yippy ki-yies" of the buyers and the sellers as the beasts were weighed and priced.[24] They would watch as the large number of well-fed cattle, sheep and hogs marched on the runways towards the smokestacks of the yards.

The constant pounding of animal footsteps shook Engine 59's one bay, two story brick firehouse located at 826 W. Exchange Avenue (about 42nd and Halsted), perfectly located to guard the pen area and the northern half of the stockyards, as well as the residential area east of Halsted Street. The firefighters used Halsted Street as a way to respond to areas around the stockyards and the Back of the Yards neighborhood and as a means to avoid delays caused by cattle drives on the smaller roads.

The 20-year-old firehouse, known as the "Liberty Engine House" was 25-by-75 feet—it was named after the

Shadows of Chicago

Liberty fire engine housed in their quarters—the costliest and mightiest engine at the time. It was purchased by The Big Three Meat Barons with the assumption it could put out any fire, anywhere in the yards.

Next to the cleaned, polished "super" engine, stood two powerful horses ready and waiting for the well-oiled harnesses to drop down on them from the ceiling onto their thick necks, allowing them to bolt out the bay door, carrying the heavy engine behind them. It was imperative that the firefighters accepted only the best horses for the firehouse. To ensure they brought in the best, the probationary firehouse horses were tested with several-mile run, often during punishing weather, all the while lugging a heavy load behind them. It was the ability to lug a heavy load that was the animal's true test, because the weight of the engines could break down some of the youngest and strongest horses. On average, firehouse horses wouldn't make it more than nine months, with only a few lasting years.[25]

Once the most impressive horses arrived at their new home, they came with a designated number, like 459 or 287. Soon though, it wouldn't take long for the horse to be given a nickname like Lightning or Sunny, or given proper names like Steve or Mary—some of the firemen named their horses after their wives or mothers-in-laws—one was even named Linsky, after a local serial killer.

At Engine 59's quarters it was the least-senior firefighter's duty to make sure the horses were newly shoed, bathed, and curried. It was not uncommon for a horse to bite and kick the young firefighters, and so to keep the horses in line, like in most other firehouses at the time, the men kept Dalmatians to calm the uneasy horses. For reasons unknown, the Dalmatian was the best dog breed for calming restless horses in the firehouse. Strangely enough, it was a usual sight to see the dogs sleeping in hay bedding right next to the horses. But contrary to their nature around the horses, the Dalmatians were not even-tempered, meek, or docile creatures as many believe they were. Instead, they were unusually strong for their size, very aggressive, and quick, and when they were not soothing the horses, they were busy killing mice, rats and other rodents, or they were stealing every morsel of food off the firehouse floor.[26]

The firefighters also preferred the Dalmation breed because they wildly barked at any stranger passing by the firehouse, and when the bay door "tripped" open, the dogs took off, sprinted in front of the firehouse, and let out a shrill bark that sounded like a siren.[27] As the engine departed the firehouse, the Dalmatians dashed along the side of the running horses until engine arrived at the scene of the fire. On scene, the dogs often sat casually by the horses, calmly waiting until it was time to go back.

Quite fittingly, the firefighters at Engine 59 were known as the "watchdogs of the yards," because they were a line of defense against emergencies that would arise in the stockyards. On the other hand, Engine 59 firefighters referred to their firehouse as the "liveliest place in the yards." They named it this because, despite the persistent stable aroma, and the firehouse's awkward location nestled amongst the stockyard pens, it was a fun place to hang out with the boys to eat, drink, play cards, tell stories, and most importantly, laugh a lot. Plus, the men didn't have much action at night, so they were often times able to sneak upstairs to the bunkroom to get a few winks before being relieved the following morning from the next platoon. In addition, there were only 50 confirmed fires up until November, which was considerably less than other firehouses around the city dealt with that year.[28]

The Engine 59 "watchdogs" were Captain Patrick Collins, Lieutenant Charles Berkery, and firefighters Peter Kill, James Foster, John Behrens, James O'Brien, Henry Cannon, William Daley, William Weber, and Frank Walters. Walters was the senior firefighter in the house, and with 27 years on the job, he was set to retire on January 1st and spend the rest of his days with his wife, Jennie. The least senior member Weber, had six years and was about to move in to a new house with his family.

Besides the firefighters and officers, Second Assistant Fire Marshal William J. Burroughs also stayed at Engine 59's quarters. Burroughs was 47, had 26 years on the job, and had received five honorable mentions for heroic acts, two of which came from rescuing men by jumping in the Chicago River. Like his only superior on the fire department, Big Jim Horan, he received yearly promotions until he became the second ranking member. He had several opportunities to take the top job, and when Mayor Edward Dunne (Busse's predecessor) asked him to accept it, he responded sharply, "I'd prefer to keep out of politics. I don't want the job. I am satisfied with my position and I love my work. I don't care to take a chance of being removed later."[29]

He loved spending time with the men at the firehouse, and especially with his wife, Belle, and their 11-year-old daughter, Helen. But the job was not the same as it used to be for him. A month before, he was injured at a fire at the Swift Meat Plant, when an axe, not belonging to any firefighter, mysteriously fell from the top of one of the lumber piles, severing much of his hand. The possible career-ending injury wasn't the worst part of it all. As a result of the severing, possibly due to an unclean axe, the exposed bone and flesh became so infected that doctors expected him to die from blood poisoning. But, being the man he was, he would regain much of his health back and return to duty days after being released from the hospital.[30]

He admitted to his family that before the mysterious axe incident he never thought about the dangerous side of his work. But now, he was more wary of his dangerous job, particularly because he was nestled next to the stockyards. He knew there was a reason why the stockyard owners positioned the Second Assistant Fire Marshal amongst the yard "watchdogs."

To The Big Three Meat Barons the Engine 59 watchdogs and Marshal Burroughs were their most important possessions. They had proven themselves as the best line of defense against major fires in the yards, and the smaller fires were usually extinguished by the yard's two large fire brigades, even before the CFD could lay out a charged hose. On top of that, the packinghouses provided watchmen 24/7 to walk up and down the pens and continually take watch of the packinghouse's floors. If an emergency were to arise, they'd break the glass on one of the 598 call boxes or "snap boxes." This would immediately send an alarm to a private fire brigade and the CFD. Besides the adequate foot patrols, there were plenty of 2 ½-inch standpipe connections for immediate support.

The problem was that the connections were inadequately supported from the water mains below. The more seasoned firefighters knew that the small mains could not protect the yards from a major fire.

*   *   *   *

That November 1910, for The Big Three Meat Barons the necessity of a high-pressure system was the least of their concerns. Their biggest concern on their plate was a chance each of them could face a year in government prison.

On September 12, 1910, they and another seven of the nation's "big men" of the meat industry were indicted for combination/conspiracy, and monopoly. The first charge, combination/conspiracy, alleged that Swift, Morris, and Armour used the National Packing Company "as a medium of their operations, the Swift, Armour, and Morris interests holding stock therein—70,000 and 50,000 and 20,000 shares respectively." The second charge, monopoly, alleged that they exploited the "field of competition by purchasing stock in that corporation until the control of it had been attained."

At first there were rumors that the indictments would be returned, just as they had been in 1905, when they were tried under similar circumstances. Before, their indictment was declared void by Judge Kenesaw Mountain Landis because he said the allegations did not violate any "beef trust."[31] This was a big win for the packers, since Judge Landis had a reputation as being one of the toughest judges in the country, and he had just let them go scot-free.

This time, after hours of deliberation, the grand jury relayed to the court that they could not arrive at a verdict. As a result of the jury's indecision, the 10 packers and their lawyers were smiling, because it meant that the charges would be washed as they had been in the past. But their smiles diminished once Judge Landis announced, "And let a special venue be drawn for a grand jury that charges against individuals in the packing business."[32]

Now that The Big Three would be investigated on an individual basis they would no longer be granted immunity because they represented one giant conglomerate. Rather, each individual packing company would remain under the constant watchful eye of Judge Landis's investigation team, all the while knowing that jail time could be in their future.

---

[1] Kolomay, Marion. *Account of the Great Stockyard Fire.*

[2] Cronon, William. *Nature's Metropolis: Chicago and the Great West.* New York: W.W. Norton & Company, 1995.

[3] *Ibid.*

[4] The Union Stockyards got its name because the area was used to provide food for the Union troops during the Civil War. It was situated several miles west of Camp Douglass, where more than six thousand Confederate soldiers had died in captivity.

[5] The boundaries stretched from 39th Street south to 47th Street, and from Halsted Street west to Ashland Avenue. It spread some 450 acres, including 13,000 animal compounds, 300 hundred miles of track, 25

miles of road, a 50 mile sewer network, 95 miles of pipe and 10,000 water hydrants.

⁶ Rice, John. *Research Data, 1910 Stockyards Fire,* November 28, 2001.

⁷ *Ibid.*

⁸ The meat monopoly pioneers of the Chicago Union Stockyards, Nelson Morris, Philip Armour, and Gustavus Swift came from humble beginnings. Morris was a poor German immigrant, unable to speak English when he took his first stockyard job cleaning pens. Armour was a ditch digger who decided to move from New York in a wagon across The Great Plains to make his vision a reality. Swift began by slaughtering animals with his own two hands and selling it house-to-house.

⁹ D'eramo, Marco. *Pig and the Skyscrapper. Chicago: A History of our Future.* New York: New Left Books, 2002.

¹⁰ Miller, Donald L. *City of the Century. The Epic of Chicago and the Making of America.* New York: Simon and Schuster, 1996.

¹¹ D'eramo.

¹² Wade, Louise Carroll. *Chicago's Pride: The Stockyards, Packingtown, and the Environs in the Nineteenth Century.* Chicago and Urbana: University of Illinois, 1987.

¹³ *Ibid.*

¹⁴ Miller.

¹⁵ *Ibid.*

¹⁶ The Canaryville neighborhood runs south of 39th Street to 47th Street, and West of Halsted to Wentworth. Today, the neighborhood retains much of its Irish heritage. The origin of name "Canaryville" is debatable. Some say the local Irish immigrants were named after the wild canaries that ate the garbage from the neighborhood dumps. Others say the earlier settlers named the area because all the Irish brogues sounded to them like singing canaries.

¹⁷ Miller.

¹⁸ *Ibid.*

¹⁹ At one popular saloon in the Back of the Yards, "The Madhouse," a round of canned beer and lunch was a nickel.

²⁰ "Back of the Yards," *Chicago Daily Tribune,* March 25, 1906.

²¹ *Ibid.*

²² Miller.

²³ The two significant efforts to unionize in 1894 and 1904 failed because the low-paid workers were unable to form an organized group. In 1937, The Congress of Industrial Organizations' Packinghouse Workers Organizing Committee helped to successfully unify workers to improve conditions.

²⁴ Miller.

²⁵ Kolomay, Marion. *Account of the Great Stockyard Fire.*

[26] *Ibid.*

[27] Sometimes bay doors opened mechanically by a series of levers, or a foot lever under the instrument desk, or hand-operated wall levers or "trips," as they were known.

[28] Kolomay.

[29] *Ibid.*

[30] "Burroughs Known As Hero For Rescues In Many Fires," *Chicago Daily Tribune,* December 23, 1910.

[31] Judge Kenesaw Mountain Landis was named after the place where his father was wounded during the Civil War. Landis was known as an ardent patriot, a staunch judge, and eventually became baseball's first commissioner in 1920.

[32] "Indicts Packers As Individuals on Three Counts: Armour, Three Swifts, Edward Morris Among Those Named in True Bills," *Chicago Daily Tribune,* September 13, 1910.

Chapter 12

THE THANKSGIVING WARNING

November 24, 1910

Big Jim leaned forward so William Moore and Joe Mackey could hear about the tragedy he foresaw in his dreams. They knew their fire marshal feared his men would die at the Chicago Union Stockyards someday, but they no longer paid much attention to his premonitions or took them seriously. Besides, at that moment it was more important they arrive at the Swift Meat Company as quickly as possible.

He knew that near the Swift factory there were not enough engine companies or fire hydrants to suppress a large scale fire. The few hydrants that did exist were supported by underground water mains too small in diameter to provide the elevated hose pressure required to protect him and his men. As a result, oils, ammonia, salt brine, and other combustibles were all waiting to be ignited from inside the walls.

Big Jim sat in the back seat of the black 1906 Buick touring car, the only motorized vehicle in the Chicago Fire Department, as it rattled and coughed light-gray smoke along the brick road. The 52-horsepower machine was equipped with leather seats, bumper-mounted spare tires, a leather convertible top, a windshield without rain wipers, and a hand-crank for a starter. He disliked the crude metal creature he ordered four years before but found that it was the quickest way to get from his quarters at city hall to any fires in town. If he had to travel only a few blocks he preferred the horse-drawn buggy. When the automobile was the best option, he chose two firemen to make sure it

Shadows of Chicago

was able to make it through all weather conditions. William Moore was the experienced driver and mechanic, while Joe Mackey served as back-up driver.[1]

On the way to the stockyards, Big Jim looked out the open roof as the small family dwellings gave way to dreary brick, windowless buildings. The tree-lined landscape turned bare as the automobile eventually made its way underneath the carved-stone steer sculpture atop the stone entrance gates of the stockyards. The gates were recently crafted by famed architects Daniel Burnham and John Root. As the car sped toward the Swift Plant they crossed over Bubbly Creek, an arm extending from the Chicago River. The 30 miles of drains and ditches derived its nickname from the fermented waste that constantly percolated to the top. Some called it "the river of death."

On this day he noticed that the cloudy sky was made even darker by the black oily smoke that coughed from the smoke stacks. As they came closer, Big Jim could taste the air of Packingtown—the rotting smell of burning flesh—a smell he knew too well. At that moment he wished he was with Margaret, his wife of seven years, and his four children, preparing for Thanksgiving dinner. However, as First Fire Marshal, Big Jim Horan had to respond to the extra-alarm fire.

The black Buick buggy slid to a halt on matted dirt in front of the burning lard building at the Swift Meat Company.[2] The warehouse was located at 42nd Street and Loomis Avenue, just two blocks south of the Nelson Morris Plant. As Big Jim made his way to the fire staging area, a safe distance in front of the warehouse, many ceased what they were doing to stare at the impressive-looking, 51-year-old First Fire Marshal. He stood between 6'2" and 6'4"—the rubber hipper boots he wore adding an extra two inches.[3] His tall frame was packed with over 200 pounds of mostly muscle. Covering his large build were a sleek black, shiny raincoat and a smoked-white leather chief's helmet. Below the rim of his helmet his blue-gray eyes were fixed on the scene ahead as he walked stoically past the dozens of fire engines, trucks, horses, and firemen.

The men parted, like Moses and the Red Sea, out of respect for their leader. His serious demeanor surprised them, because he normally approached fire scenes with humor to calm them. For example, Big Jim would often refer himself in the third person: he'd say, "Horan's going to fight the fire today." He used his frequent abnormal speech to divert attention away from himself and it satisfied him when firefighters would laugh at or mimic it, for he knew it was important to relax the battle-ready men before they risked their lives.

After Big Jim arrived at the staging area outside the Swift warehouses, he immediately walked up to Second Assistant Fire Marshal William Burroughs to better assess where the fire had spread and if the firemen were making any progress. As Burroughs relayed the dire details while pointing in the direction of the fire, Big Jim couldn't ignore Burrough's missing hand—now just a sewed-up stump near his wrist—it was severed just weeks earlier at another Swift Warehouse fire

Burroughs, now back to active duty, informed Big Jim about the complex situation at the Swift factories. As Big Jim viewed the scene, he noticed the three buildings within feet of each other—two buildings were five story brick structures, the other, a four story wooden frame storehouse. What immediately captured his attention was the dark smoke billowing from one of the five-story buildings that housed the factory where soft, white lard was made from animal carcasses. This concerned him because if this fire continued to rage, the other building as well as the storehouse would incinerate in minutes because, unlike the burning building, the other two exposure buildings housed the factories that contained the explosive chemicals added to lard to remove impurities.

Shadows of Chicago

Big Jim ordered most of the men to attack the interior of the burning structure to stop the fire from burning out of control and to protect the two exposure buildings from radiated heat and direct flames. Others were ordered to stay outside in case the flames jumped to either building. To prevent this he called for a total of 22 engine companies, four truck companies, and several private companies to prevent the fire from spreading. The private firemen were employed by stockyard owners to slow the spread of the fire before Chicago companies arrived and to lower insurance costs for owners—owners were rewarded with lower premiums if they hired the private firemen, or "watchmen" as they were called, to patrol the yards 24 hours at a time.

After Big Jim guided the men to their tasks, he walked over to the fire engines to check the gauges to see if they provided sufficient water for the men advancing the hose lines. He was pleased the engine gauges indicated enough water pumping from the hydrants connected to the water mains below; however, he remained concerned that the mains were too small in diameter to provide adequate water if the other two buildings caught fire.

Seeing there was sufficient water for the moment, Big Jim tracked hundreds of feet of charged hose lines into the burning building to reach the men behind the nozzles to assess the progress. He used one particular hose line as a trail through numerous dark recesses and rooms—flames gnawed through the brick on both sides of him—the smoky air dense as a satin curtain. As smoke became progressively worse, he lowered his head and puffed short breaths to adapt to the oxygen-deficient air, eventually arriving at Engine 59 advancing the charged nozzle. The men at the hose were reassured to have their trusted fire marshal now guiding their way.

Engine 59 was the first company on the scene at 11:00 a.m. and fought the most brutal fight in the belly of

Matthew Drew

the burning factory. Captain Patrick Collins and pipemen Frank Walters, William Weber, and William Daley advanced through the pitch-dark hallways—crouching lower than the thick smoke blanket above them—taking turns breathing fresh oxygen and wetting their mouths from the gushing hose nozzle. They were assisted by Truck 11; Lieutenant Herman Brandenberg and truckmen Nicholas Crane, Peter Powers, and Albert Moriarty swung their axes and yanked pike poles to expose hidden fire in the walls, floors, and ceilings.[4]

As first-arriving company members, Engine 59 and Truck 11 knew to remain in the fire building until every glowing ember was drenched—this was a rarely-mentioned, unwritten rule for all firemen—it was shameful to back away from a burning structure unless it was obvious lives were in peril. Plus, they also knew they could not back out until Big Jim signaled for them to pick up their equipment.

By 5:00 p.m., once Big Jim was satisfied that the fire was washed of all visible embers and the other five-story building and storehouse appeared to be spared from the fire, the exhausted first-arriving firemen were ordered to again drown the entire structure so the fire would not rekindle; meanwhile, the additional companies were relieved so they could enjoy part of the Thanksgiving holiday.

Big Jim directed Engine 59, Engine 52, Truck 11, Truck 18, and private firefighters to stay behind during the final walk-through of the three Swift buildings before they picked up the equipment.[5] He directed Captain Patrick Collins of Engine 59 and his tired men to check the other five story building to look for fire spread—others checked the four story wooden storeroom.

Just as Collins and his pipemen rushed out to tell Big Jim the fire had communicated to the upper floors of the five-story exposure building (possibly by way of chemical fumes or radiated heat), the roof burst open—

flames bolted out the roof and top floor windows—lighting up the late evening sky. Just as glass, tar, and roof boards rained at Big Jim's feet, he called for the relieved companies to return.

Big Jim could not wait for the support to arrive because he found that the fire had quickly spread to the four-story wooden storehouse. Before he could gather the few available men to fight the five-story brick building and the storehouse, Chicago Fireman Louis Mallory told him that Fire Marshal John Juday, head of the private fire patrol, became trapped behind a wall of fire near the entrance of the storehouse. Big Jim shouted for a "Mayday"—the men knew this meant to halt firefighting efforts to concentrate on the trapped firefighter.

Big Jim turned around and yelled, "Come on, boys!"

He grabbed Engine 59, the nearest company to him, to follow him with a charged hose, and as soon as they attempted to step inside the storehouse, they were hurled back by an explosion caused by greasy fumes and the gases mixing in the oxygen from the ventilators. Big Jim, again trying to lead the pipemen through the entrance, held his breath while throwing his body through the searing flames so his lungs would not burn; the rest of the men followed with their charged hose. Once successfully inside the building, all the rescuers stood behind the hose as it did little to relinquish heat and flames—the hose pressure was futile against the chemical-soaked storehouse—when there was sufficient water pressure earlier in the first factory. The chemicals added to the lard increased the heat of fire and allowed it to slither its way through the rooms easily.

Big Jim decided to continue further into the storehouse alone so no one else became trapped like Juday. Seconds after he took a few steps, another explosion sent him off his feet, and as he sat shaken-up in the near darkness, he noticed something unusual had fallen into his hands. He wiped the stinging ash and embers from his eyes to focus on the missing chief's helmet—the explosion had tossed Chief Juday's helmet and indicated he lay nearby. Big Jim crawled several feet more until he found the chief's body trapped face-down under a giant door and other debris.

It was too dangerous for Big Jim to check the fallen chief, for he ate too much smoke and the storehouse was about to be a fully-involved fire.[6] He was forced to tow Juday's limp body until he reached his men at the storeroom entrance. Just when they were all about to exit the same fire wall they entered, another small explosion sent heavy timber slamming in front of them, trapping them in a fiery prison.

Upon realizing their men trapped, Truck 11, Truck 18, and others frantically slashed their axes through the burning wood from outside the storehouse. Charles Moore and Nicholas Doyle, best friends on Truck 18, were the first to carve gaps through the blocked entrance. Inside the newly carved openings, Truck 11 was able to drive pry bars to remove the flaming timber from the doorway. The men heaved the gasping firemen out of the storehouse when there was a large enough opening. Just as Big Jim and the trapped men took their first breaths of fresh air, the entire entrance section of the storehouse blasted fire like an enormous furnace; the fire came within several inches of where the men lay breathless.

Big Jim pulled his worn body over to Marshall Juday to check his condition. He looked into the chief's blank eyes, knowing he was dead. The more Big Jim stared into his lifeless eyes the more he knew it could have been his men or him lying there.

Big Jim turned his head to check on the rest of the firemen—relieved to find them wiping soot from their eyes and hacking ash from their throats. He directed medical personnel to attend to most injured; Captain Patrick Collins, William Weber, Frank Walters and William Daley

Shadows of Chicago

of Engine 59, along with truckmen Nicholas Doyle, Nicholas Crane, and Charles Moore had to be treated at the hospital for smoke inhalation. Big Jim and the rest of the men refused medical treatment even though their red eyes dripped soot and their chests burned; instead, they joined Burroughs and the fresh engine companies until they drowned what little remained of the three Swift buildings. They all stood several feet from the remaining five-story, wobbling brick walls.

Big Jim was told later, not surprisingly, that the cause of the fire was spontaneous combustion—but that's what all reports said after every stockyard fire.

---

[1] Kolomay, Marion. *Account of the Great Stockyard Fire.*

[2] Even after fire department vehicles became motorized, chiefs' autos were still called "buggies."

[3] Hippers were fire boots that ran up the legs, just short of the hips.

[4] The pike poles, usually six feet in length, have a sharp metal hook at the end. The strange looking tool is still effective in exposing hidden fire from unreachable positions.

[5] Every major fire requires that officers assess entire perimeters before evacuating fire scenes. This is known commonly as the "final walk-through." Engine and Truck companies remain to prevent another fire outbreak.

[6] A "fully-involved" fire is usually considered a lost cause for a structure and its contents. The preferred method to fighting a fully-involved fire is to "surround and drown," a defensive tactic involving all available firefighters to drench the remaining fuel.

Chapter 13

THE GREAT STOCKYARD FIRE

December 22, 1910

On December 21, 1910, during the city council meeting, Big Jim stood tall before the members as he described the events of the Thanksgiving fire to prove that stockyards were "a fire trap," and how the unnecessary death of Fire Marshal Juday was due to the council's inability to act.

He wished he had his old friend Freddy Busse in his corner, but he was out of state on a business trip. Maybe he wouldn't be much help anyways, since he never was able to push through the high-pressure system. Instead, Big Jim stood alone, facing the council and reporters as his blood boiled.

He argued that for eight long years the high-pressure issue sat idly on their tables, and how any large-scale fire in the stockyards would leave surrounding communities, like the Back of the Yards neighborhood, "practically bare of companies." This made the entire city vulnerable to a wide-scale fire like the Grain Elevator Fire, or worse, The Great Chicago Fire. Finding his composure he added, "Chicago has had her lesson, but the present generation seems to have forgotten it. Is it wise to wait for a second Chicago fire, where means of preventing it are available?"

As Big Jim spoke, an alderman interrupted him, saying that it was more important that a high-pressure system be placed in the downtown district. Big Jim's face went beet-red with anger and blurted out that he "didn't give a damn how the buildings were in the downtown district," but what was needed was better protection in the stockyards. He continued with his tirade, saying that all that he hears from the council is "lack of funds," when the extra protection would cost $3 million, not an extravagant amount considering the savings down the road.

He also presented to the council a detailed plan. It entailed working together with stockyard owners to install a water plant capable of supporting the high-pressure system. Unfortunately, neither the city council nor the stockyard owners would ever act on the measures, and Big Jim's final forewarning to the city council meeting met with deaf ears, just as it always had.[1]

At 4:30 that evening, he signed the final documents that would allow fire department members to help create children's skating rinks around the city. He left the signed documents on his desk and exited his office for the day. There to meet him curbside in front of City Hall was his driver and mechanic, Firefighter William Moore. He asked if Moore could drive him around the city to talk to chiefs about his displeasure with the city council that day, and maybe have a few laughs to forget about his trying day. After his last visit with Chief Michael Corrigan, Moore took Big Jim to his home on 722 South Ashland Avenue at 10:30 p.m.

Moore headed back his quarters at Engine 103 at Harrison and Laflin streets. Once he pulled put his automobile away for the night, he hit the bunkroom for a little shut-eye.[2]

* * * *

In the early morning on December 22, 1910, Paul Leskie, the 38-year-old night watchman for the Nelson Morris Company, was ready to go home. It was 4:00 a.m., it was below freezing outside, and his night shift was about to end. All night long he had walked through the each of the meat packing plants to see if anything was out of the ordinary.

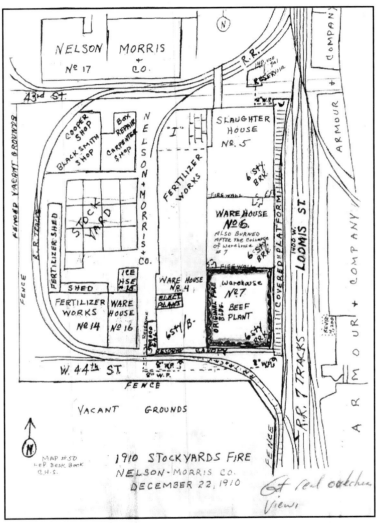

1910 Stockyards Fire. Illustration by Nelson-Morris Co., 1910. Courtesy of John Rice.

Shadows of Chicago

Someone was assigned to make sure the night watchmen wouldn't doze off, and as an added measure an IDT watchman signal box/time clock had to be pulled every 10 minutes. He was also required to check in with fellow watchmen Andrew Dzurman and Patrick Reaph. Dzurman spent much of the shift instructing Reaph on the rules of the packing plant. Reaph, the newcomer on the job, was only 23 and he had just come from Ireland with his sister.

Although the watchmen's primary job was to look for any maintenance trouble within the factory, they were also trained as firefighters through the Morris Fire Brigade. Even though each had little fire experience, most watchmen knew that the meat packing factories could easily catch fire, especially Warehouse Seven, also known as the Beef House; it contained pickled meat, saltpeter, and salt brine—all flammable and highly explosive.

Warehouse Seven was a six-story solid brick, windowless structure, except for a single row of iron-shuttered windows. A 15-foot-wide platform ran parallel to the width of the building from which butchered meat could be loaded out the freight house doors onto refrigerated rail cars lined along the platform—the meat was shipped and then sold throughout the country. A wood canopy hung over the loading dock and railcars to protect workers from the weather. Further east on Loomis Street was a line of box cars and seven sets of tracks, separating Armour and Morris meat packing plants. There were two exposed walls, facing the south and the east. To the north was Warehouse Six, and to the west Warehouse Four. Both were six stories and separated from Warehouse Seven only by a brick firewall.

As soon as Paul Leskie entered Warehouse Seven, he smelled burnt meat. Following the scent, he ran down several stairs into the basement and then opened the door to the hide storage room. The odor was stronger, and a gray smoky haze drifted along the ceiling. To further investigate he walked through aisles of cow hides hanging on hooks, all

Matthew Drew

the while the smell of burning animal skin grew stronger. As he continued to follow the stench, a rush of flames and dark black smoke drove him back, sending him off his feet. He crawled for a moment to stay low from the heat and the pungent smoke above. He left the hide room door open and dashed for the stairs going up from the basement as the fire ran along the grease-soaked floors. He ran over to Warehouse Six and pulled the A.D.T. fire alarm box.[3] This notified the Stockyard Fire Brigade and the fire alarm office to send more response units.

By this time the fire had leapt through the open door of the hide room and torched the rest of the basement. For a moment Leskie reentered the burning building, looking for his fellow watchmen, Andrew Dzurman and Patrick Reaph, but he was driven back out of the warehouse by the heavy black smoke, making it impossible to find them.[4]

*   *   *   *

The firefighter on duty at the joker stand notified Truck 11 that they would soon be called to the Morris Plant, so they hit the floor in anticipation.[5] Their single bay door opened, letting in the freezing morning air. Simultaneously, the harnesses lowered onto their horses, and their skinny Dalmatian ran out the bay doors and barked on the street to clear traffic, even though the street was deserted.

The men of Truck 11 were only hours away from being relieved by the next shift.[6] They spent much of the night getting in the Christmas mood. They all had much to celebrate. It was Edward Schonsett's 27th birthday and the next day would be his third anniversary. To begin the celebration his wife, Minnie, would have breakfast on the table as soon as he got back home. Lieutenant Herman Brandenberg was working on his day off so he could spend Christmas with his family. Albert Moriarty's brothers, George and William, both professional baseball players

Shadows of Chicago

(George played 3rd base on Ty Cobb's Detroit Tigers), were visiting him for the holidays from their training in Cuba, both carried fine cigars for their brother Al and the rest of Truck 11. Nicholas Doyle was ready to spend Christmas with his fire family; at the time, there were enough Doyles in the Chicago Fire Department to fill an entire firehouse. Actually, Nick's father, Captain Dennis Doyle of Engine 39, was already in route to the call. The rest of the men from Truck 11 Peter Powers, Claus Clausen, and Michael McInerney were also anxious to celebrate Christmas with their families, not knowing they were about to fight the greatest battle of their lives.[7]

* * * *

The first companies to Warehouse Seven were Engines 39, 49, 52, 53, 59, and Trucks 18 and 33, along with Chief Martin Lacy of the Eleventh Battalion, taking charge as incident commander. After a quick size-up of the situation, he directed Engine 53, the first pumper with a charged line, to direct water into the heavy black smoke pouring from the first-floor freight service doors. Once the line was fully opened, the insufficient stream did little to slow the expanding beast hiding behind the freight doors.

When Second Assistant Fire Marshall William Burroughs arrived, he took control of the scene. As he assumed position atop the loading dock to direct the men, he noticed that most of the horses and the steamers had to stop to the east of the seven rows of tracks, staying by the hydrants—many as far as a hundred feet from Morris Warehouse Seven. He watched as dozens of firefighters raced in all directions, lugging tangled lines over the railroad tracks and under box cars.

As Burroughs surveyed the scene, he eyed the possible danger the exposure buildings may pose. From the west of Warehouse Seven, was a small building, separated only by a firewall. To the north, there was another adjoining building, but this one was seven stories high and hundreds of feet long. To the south, there was six-story windowless building a good distance away from Warehouse Seven. Seeing no other option but to attack the building from the south and the east, Burroughs told the engine companies to direct hose lines from the vantage point of the railroad tracks and a platform.

Burroughs directed Lacy to inform him of any changes in the fire. The firefighters felt comfortable having both Burroughs and Lacy as chief officers, especially for their knowledge of cold storage buildings explosive under fire conditions. No one knew the danger more than Lacy, whose memory of the Columbian Exposition Fire still haunted him.[8]

Lacy yelled for Charles Moore and Nicholas Crane of Truck 18 to hack holes through the wooden freight doors, and for the Engine 59 "watchdogs" to follow with a solid water stream so that every time the fire attempted to grab oxygen from outside the warehouse, a water line would drown it. When William Weber, driver for Engine 59, sent the water through his connected pumper, water drizzled out the pipe. It would take another 12 minutes before a solid water line was on the fire, for it was discovered that the private fire companies shut down the water mains that fed the hydrants to avoid freezing.

Once the mains were opened and the hoses bulged with liquid ammunition, the fire companies made their first true offensive charge toward the enemy.

"Go...Go...Go," said Captain Collins of Engine 59, as one hand pointed to the freight doors, the other hand waved for Frank Walters and William Weber to advance the line.

The men stuck to their post, focusing their stream through the opening, but suddenly, the fire had gained too much momentum and the smoke and heat became too intense. The conditions drove the men back to the canopy and the boxcars, trapping them. Their only defense was to crouch low, breathe the least smoke as possible, and continue to shoot blindly at the fire.

Captain Dennis Doyle of Engine 39, seeing the firefighters' trapped below him from atop the loading platform, directed a second water line to relieve the companies below. The second line allowed for greater visibility, relieving the trapped men and allowing Truck 18 the ability to chop new holes in the service doors with their axes. This granted the men hope for a new offensive stance. But, just when a third line was charged to drench the newly carved opening, the water pressure dropped again.

To find out for certain why the pressure had dropped, Lieutenant Charles Berkerey of Engine 59 climbed though the boxcar couplings and back to the engine. The engines compound gauges indicated that an insignificant amount of water was being pumped from the water mains below. After Berkerey relayed the dire details to Burroughs, Burroughs ordered one line to be shut down to regain effective streams for the other two.

Meanwhile, the fire raced through interior portion of the building by means of superheated, chemically-enhanced gases traveling up from the first floor. Yet the fire revealed little to indicate its growing power within. The only evidence of its strength was that pressure from the rising heat caused it to exhale puffs of black smoke though the mortar joints of the upper floors. Recognizing this as a dangerous sign, Lacy quickly notified Burroughs. In turn, Burroughs ordered his buggy driver to activate the 4-11 alarm, the signal to notify First Fire Marshal Horan.[9]

* * * *

As firefighter William Moore slept in his firehouse bunk at Engine 103, he had a peculiar dream that he would tell later:

Matthew Drew

I dreamt that I was out in the lake in a tug boat which hit a brick wall and sunk and I was the only one saved of the many on board, and I found myself sitting on the wall which the boat collided with, when I awoke from the alarm. I immediately fell asleep again, and began to dream this time that Chief Horan's head was severed at the shoulders and was standing on the ground talking to me.

At 4:42 a.m., Moore was awoken by the 4-11 alarm that had come from Second Fire Marshal Burroughs. Although Moore was happy that he was shaken from his awful dream, he felt that there was something especially urgent about the alarm.[10]

Moore raced to meet fellow Firefighter/Driver Joe Mackey on the apparatus floor. Moore rotated the crank of the 1906 Buick, causing the 52-horsepower engine to rip-roar then settle to its idling sound. Then, Mackey and he hopped in and pushed the automobile as fast as it could go, arriving at Big Jim's home at 722 South Ashland in five minutes.

Outside of his home, Moore rang the secret bell, alerting the fire marshal in his bedroom. Big Jim answered the door in his bed clothes.

"What are you doing?" he asked.

"There's a 4-11 in the yards at 43th and Loomis," Moore said, motioning for Big Jim to get going.

When he turned around, his wife, Margaret, gazed at him.

"What's the matter, Jimmy?"

"Nothing, dear," he answered. "Just another fire."

He put on his clothes slower than usual near the front door and near the Christmas tree and gifts for his 2-year-old daughter, Ella, and 3-year-old son, William—also there was a gift for his wife, a picture of the kids together.

Once dressed, he uttered some mumbled goodbyes and hurried out the door. His wife watched him depart, and never went back to sleep, sensing something was wrong.

When Big Jim entered the automobile he said, "Horan's running a little late. You'll have to hit it up." Big Jim then said to Moore and Mackey, "Careful of the ice. We don't want an accident."

After making a few wrong turns, the three arrived at the south end of Warehouse Seven at 5:05 a.m. From their position, they could see dark smoke hovering around the warehouse, but no visible tongues of fire. Big Jim rushed towards the fire scene, while Moore stayed with the automobile for a moment, tending to the radiator to keep the water from freezing. All the while he was afraid his eerie dream was coming true.[11]

* * * *

Second Assistant Fire Marshal Burroughs, Chief Martin Lacy, and other fire officers stood atop the platform, presenting possible solutions to the deadly situation, despite the chaos around them. Even their temporary post on the platform was death trap—further complicated by the rotten wooden canopy extending over both platform and the boxcars. The men knew the platform, canopy, and box cars made a quick escape impossible, but it still provided the best means to attack from the east. The biggest problem was that the fire had most of the firefighters packed together, cramped like the cattle and hog carcasses in the refrigerator box cars next to them.

Burroughs, Lacy, and the other officers did not know that as they talked the fire had drifted up the grease-soaked walls of warehouse, weakening the connections between the floor joists and the walls of the warehouse. In addition, gas pressure was building from the burning grease and salt brine.

Matthew Drew

As Burroughs and Lacy were contemplating their next move, Big Jim walked up to the officers gathered on the platform. He face was red, and his normally happy disposition was gone. He asked, "Why isn't there more [water] pressure?" Not waiting for an answer he asked, "Why aren't those doors battered in?"

Big Jim felt that he didn't have enough time to find out why the officers were not making progress. Instead, he ordered Chief Lacy to attack the northeast part Warehouse Seven and then ordered Burroughs and Mackey to check the condition of the warehouse atop the canopy. Burroughs reluctantly agreed and two remained perched on the canopy, despite being perilously close to the warehouse's collapse zone

By this time, most knew that Big Jim was now in charge at the scene. Upon realizing this, more and more firefighters marched towards him to see how they could help. Quickly deciding what to do next, he directed Trucks 11 and 18 to use their axes and pike poles to slash holes in the freight door to expose the warehouse's fiery belly. With every chop, the fire licked their helmets, coats, and bare skin. As he watched his son Nicholas of Truck 11 and company members in trouble, Captain Dennis Doyle directed his men on Engine 39 to send a cool stream to relieve the thrashing truckmen. At the same time, Louis Mallory and Thomas Costello of Engine 29 took turns zeroing their line on the truckmen and the exposed fire furnace.

Big Jim saw that if the warehouse was not controlled it would go, and seeing that the engine companies now had solid streams, he decided to make a full charge at the fire. Just as he was ready to gather some pipemen together, Lieutenant James Fitzgerald and George Enthof of Engine 23 reported their arrival and offered to help. Additionally, he called on ever-willing Engine 59 to follow him into the main body of the fire. As always, Big Jim led the way, while

Engines 23 and 59 followed close behind, armed with charged hoses.

Meanwhile, atop the canopy Burroughs warned, "You'd better back down, Chief."

Minutes after Big Jim and his men disappeared into the smoke towards the fiery beast, they reappeared, but this time they were retreating back to the platform. No one knew for certain what they seen or heard to make them return. Some believed they heard the floors give way and pancake. If the floors pancaked, they were dropping one by one until the support walls were at the mercy of gravity.

The sight was dreadful enough for Big Jim to yell in the direction of Mackey and Burroughs, still settled on the canopy. He screamed, "Look out, men! The walls are falling!" It's amazing he had enough resolve to warn his men, when he knew it may be his last breath.

The men nearest the warehouse scurried in their confined space between the tons of the brick and the platform, trying to escape the trap. At the same time, the men to the south were also trapped. All were at the mercy of the lurching wall.

The six-story warehouse hissed, let out a "grinding sound," swayed outward 10 feet, and then sent the east wall crashing. This sent a tsunami of bricks and mortar striking with precision on the men below, almost like a giant claw. One observer said it looked like Big Jim's body was swallowed by smoke and fire.

Another observer said that Burrough's body was thrown from the canopy, somersaulted against a freight car, and was then buried under fiery rubble. The tons of bricks crushed the canopy like tissue paper, the platform was driven into the earth, and the freight cars were flung like toys onto their sides, causing the ground to quake miles away.

Mackey's body was chucked from the canopy between two freight cars and buried by scorching bricks, and hacked, burning wood. A wooden beam balanced above him, protecting him from the larger, possible life-ending debris.

Moore's body was thrown to the north after he heard the crash. When he tried to get back up to run, he was knocked unconscious by an unknown projectile.

Chief Lacy was positioned north of the fire, his back facing the warehouse. As the avalanche of bricks headed towards him, another firefighter pulled him away from the most lethal impact, but he was still buried under a pile of bricks.

Lieutenant Berkery and Captain Lannon were hurled from the north platform dozens of feet away, knocked unconscious, and then they rolled under a freight car. When Berkery came to, he rested from his injuries for two hours, and then was able to help man the hoses. Lannon was not as lucky.

The remainder of fighting men closest to Warehouse Seven were buried under six stories of scorching bricks and mortar. And as an added insult, hundreds of animal carcasses, weighing an additional thousand pounds, flopped on top of the ruins. Gusts of flaming wind followed, challenging an immediate rescue effort.[12]

* * * *

Firefighters who were not buried under the carnage were stunned for the moment, their ears still ringing. The second they came to the realization of what happened, their first instinct was to start digging for their fallen comrades.

Shadows of Chicago

One of the last known pictures of Fire Chief James "Big Jim" Horan, walking past a building at a fire; 1910; Photographer--Chicago Daily News, Inc. Chicago History Museum, #DN-0008864.

Almost at once, crowds of firefighters charged through the clouds of smoke until they reached the enormous three-story wreckage. As they started to climb and toss aside the debris, the intense heat burned their feet through their shoes and burned their hands through their gloves. Soon they all realized the hopelessness of the rescue effort.

They found that the only way they could initiate a rescue was to control the fire that still raged among the rubble. It was decided that best method was to hit the fire with hoses by surrounding it using every available vantage point. The problem with this was they required additional resources to fight the rest of the warehouse that continued to burn. The warehouse's grease-soaked wood scorched so hot, that radiant heat was threatening the surrounding structures. The problem intensified due to the low water pressure.

The situation was so dismal four special alarms were called by the Acting Chief Seyferlich.[13] Before the additional fire companies made it to the scene, another six-story building fell near the firefighters that were still fighting the first wreckage. The newly fallen building crashed, sending debris so heavy it knocked down several freight cars, luckily missing the men nearby.

Every firefighter worked nonstop, often times nowhere near their company members. This posed a problem for captains as they tried to take roll. This confusion instigated several speculations about who was missing and who was not. Some of the "missing" were presumed dead, when later they were found fighting the fire. Other assumptions turned out to be true.

Not until 11:30 a.m. were the firefighters able to assault the mound where their members went missing. Despite being beaten and tired, hundreds worked frantically to tear away at the carnage. Once they began to find evidence of the fallen men, they concentrated their search in that particular area. The rescuers first came upon Mackey, who was alive, but had a fractured leg. This gave renewed hope that others may be found alive. However, to the rescuers' dismay, several of their dead brothers were found one after another. Their lifeless bodies were reverently situated on Red Cross stretchers and covered with whatever was available to conceal their sickening-looking wounds. Any time a new body was discovered, rescue workers silently made a line, and then the bodies were passed along through the wreckage until the bodies arrived at the horrified civilians in the safe zone.

As rescuers continued their search for new victims, the south wall fell with a thunderous crash near a rescue party, raining bricks throughout much of scene. Due to the danger the surrounding structures posed, Acting Chief Seyferlich thought it would be best that he got a look from every available angle to make sure everyone was safe from falling structures before the rescue would continue. Fortunately, during his scene assessment, he found another windowless six-story building to the south of fire that had almost identical conditions to the initial fire building. Like Warehouse Seven's fire, the building's upper floors revealed intermittent puffs of black smoke.

The outside of the structure looked incapable of falling, but after further inspection, it was revealed that super-heated, chemically-induced gases caused the fire to eat away at the entire inner core of the building. This startling revelation stirred Seyferlich to rush every working firefighter completely away from the building's collapse zone. Just in time, the south warehouse crashed in the area where, just minutes before, working firefighters, rescuers, and spectators were gathered.

Some of the spectators included grief-stricken family members of the missing, curious civilians, and meat-packing workers. Standing among their workers were J. Ogden Armour, Edward Morris, and Charles and Edward

Swift. Standing next to them was Mayor Busse. At one point Busse exclaimed loudly, "Enough lives have been lost. I want no more risks taken to save a few dollars' worth of property. All the men must be kept far enough away to be out of danger of falling walls." Busse's comment revealed how frustrated he was at the unnecessary loss of firefighters, particularly his friend whose body had yet to be recovered.

Seyferlich demanded that there would not be an extensive rescue and recovery effort, because extensive fires persisted in the Morris buildings, adjacent to the ruins. Throughout the evening, flames shot from the Morris buildings as high as 200 feet in some places. As hundreds of firefighters worked furiously to put out the Morris blazes, dozens of others were in charge of stopping spreading fires before it threatened the entire stockyards and the residential areas. At one point, fires spread across Loomis Street to the Armour plant. Firefighters were able to contain it before it detonated another fast-spreading fire that the department would have been ill-equipped to handle.

Amazingly, by nightfall firefighters contained most of the newly-ignited structures, despite the ever-present low-pressure water system, and an equally difficult dilemma, the darkness. The darkness, coupled with smoke, made fire duty especially impossible. With the help of civilians and police officers, lanterns were lit, providing an added means to contain the fire. But for onlookers, the lights directed at the wreckage displayed eerie shadows on the surrounding structures.

Once the enormous ruins were mostly washed down, Seyferlich gave the okay to continue the body recovery operation. Since most of the firefighters were worn out and still busy washing hot spots, police officers were called in to aid in the search.

Again, body after body of lifeless firefighters was pulled from the wreckage. One of the deceased was that of

Shadows of Chicago

Nicholas Doyle, the son of Dennis Doyle. This realization caused a hush to fall upon the crowd, since they were beholding proof of double-family tragedy.

Another body took the rescuers by surprise. Edward Schonsett's body was intact, except that his right arm was severed. When rescuers went to place the arm on his body, they were stunned to realize his lifeless hand was still clinging tightly to an axe.

It took until 9:35 p.m. that the body of Chief Horan was found about 15 feet from where the fallen wall had once stood. First someone spotted his white chief's helmet, causing others to search in the area at feverish pace. When rescuers came upon his body, he was sitting, his face bent forward with his arms folded over his chest. He body was covered in pulverized brick dust. A heavy beam held his leg below the knee, nearly severing it. The back of his skull was fractured, indicating that his death was quick. The most incredible detail was that face was entirely free from blemishes, and he had an almost serene look on his face.

Silence went over the crowd as his fellow brothers lifted him Big Jim on the Red Cross stretcher. Then, someone slowly placed their black poncho on top of his enormous body. This signaled the procession to carry his body three blocks to a waiting ambulance. All the while his men saluted their leader as he passed.

At 10:30 p.m. the last body was removed from the wreckage, Lieutenant James Fitzgerald, was easily identified by the company designation on his helmet. Others bodies were much harder to identify, like Stephen Leen, a 19-year-old clerk for the Morris Company. It was found much later that Leen was busy tagging freight cars, when he stopped (to close) to watch the men fight the fire.

After all the bodies were removed from the debris, and in face of all the horror that had befallen the firefighters on the scene, they still continued to put out spreading fires through the stockyards until the following evening. Another

37 fought to get well in the hospital. Two would eventually die later, Captain Lannon and Pipeman Walters.

In the morning papers around the country people were given the names of 21 Chicago firefighters and three others who fought bravely and died at the Chicago Union Stockyards and afterwards. Of the deceased were three members of Engine 59, six of the seven members of Truck 11, and a father and son.[14]

---

[1] "Death of Horan to Bring Reform of Water System?," *Chicago Daily Tribune*: December 23, 1910.

[2] Kolomay, Marion. *Account of the Great Stockyard Fire.*

[3] The Stockyards provided A.D.T fire alarm boxes throughout all the factories to alert private companies and the nearest Chicago engine company. They were meant to lower insurance costs.

[4] "23 Killed in Fire at Packing Plant; Chief Horan Dead," *Chicago Daily Tribune,* December 23, 1910.

[5] One firefighter was always supposed the stand ready listen at the "joker stand" to listen to ticker of the fire alarm box. "To hit the floor," means to get ready for a working fire. Good fires at the Stockyards always required additional companies.

[6] Chicago Firefighters were on a two-shift system, which meant they had twenty-four hours of rest before the next shift.

[7] Kolomay.

[8] The World's Columbian Exposition was extravagant fair that took place in Chicago in 1893. At the fair's cold storage facility, in front of horrified spectators, a fire caused the death of fourteen firefighters.

[9] This was the very first 4-11 call in the history of the fire department. Almost three quarters of the department had to respond.

[10] Kolomay.

[11] *Ibid.*

[12] "23 Killed in Fire at Packing Plant; Chief Horan Dead," *Chicago Daily Tribune,* December 23, 1910.

[13] Chief Charles Seyferlich was Third Assistant Fire Marshal before the fire. He took command of the stockyard fire because First Marshal Horan and Second Assistant Fire Marshal Burroughs were missing.

[14] "23 Killed in Fire at Packing Plant; Chief Horan Dead," *Chicago Daily Tribune,* December 23, 1910.

Shadows of Chicago

Chapter 14

BIG JIM'S SPIRIT FIGHTS ON

The day after the stockyard fire, Mayor Busse called for an emergency session at the city council. After members of the council took their seats, he slowly took his place before them as his head bowed towards the floor. The council members couldn't help but notice how visibly distraught he was. His eyes were reddened from the tears he shed and because he didn't sleep at all that night. On top of that, his face was still slightly blackened from the smoke he endured the day before. He choked back the tears that were beginning to swell again. Then to his humbled audience, he muttered, "It was an awful catastrophe. I am simply heartsick over it all. Jim Horan I had known him since we were five-year-old boys together, and no man did I admire more than him. He was a firefighter through and through and a man that was a man... Jim came to my home frequently and I admired him greatly. I feel sorry for his family and the firemen who died at the call of duty. He was one of the most efficient officials in the city's service and possessed wonderful executive ability. He was also one of the bravest men that has ever been connected to the fire department."[1]

After Mayor Busse's opening statement he relayed to the council the bizarre details of how he found out about the stockyard fire. He said it was 8:00 a.m. and was returning to Chicago from Kansas. He picked up the morning paper and was reading details about a December 21st Philadelphia fire that killed a number of firefighters. At that moment he was thinking of his friend Jim, and thought *thank heavens the same thing was not happening in Chicago.* When he looked up from his paper, a reporter from *The Daily News*, who also happened to also be a passenger on the train, said he had some bad news for him. He passed on to the Busse that he just found out that Marshal Horan and his men were buried under six-story wall at that the stockyards. The reporter said that after hearing the news, "The mayor sat silent, gazing out the window for several minutes. The tears came to his eyes and he quietly wiped them away. The muscles in his jaws tightened as he pressed his lips together to control his feeling." Busse gazed at the reporter and stammered, "Jim and I were boys together… There wasn't a day that we were off that we were not together. I knew his friends in the department and his enemies. He was tolerant of the latter, more so than I would have been."[2]

Firefighters crowded below the spot where Jim Horan's body and others were found at the Nelson Morris and Company stockyards fire; 1910. Chicago History Museum, #DN-0056350.

Matthew Drew

When their train arrived at the station, he and the *The Daily News* reporter rushed to the scene of the fire. According to the reporter, the second the automobile pulled up to stockyard entrance Busse jumped out and "plunged into the smoke and through water, snow, and a network of pipes on foot. Under the viaduct near Loomis Street, the smoke from the fire and the snorting engines was so dense that a party could only grope blindly ahead."

Busse next told the council how after hours of waiting to see the fate of his friend, he was told that that the recovery efforts would have to wait several hours until the dangerous conditions were controlled. At that, several people dragged him away from the scene to grab a cup of coffee and a sandwich. Then, he went to his office downtown to gather his thoughts. After several hours, he was contacted at City Hall and told that Big Jim's body was taken to the undertaker's shop. The shop was owned by Big Jim's brother, Daniel Horan.

At 11:00 p.m., Busse picked up his wife, Josephine, and sped to the undertaker's. Once there, moving through dozens of mourners he hollered, "Where's the body?" No one answered, but they pointed to his lifeless body on a slab covered with a sheet. He walked slowly over to his old friend, grabbed his lifeless hand and said, "Poor Jim! Poor Jim!" Busse could say no more. He just wiped away his tears; his large-framed body shook, and he walked away to the corner of the undertaking and began to cry alone. Once he regained his composure, he walked over to join the other mourners. Big Jim's wife Margaret was not one of the mourners; instead, she sent this plea from their home: "Send 'Jim' home tonight. No matter how he is, send him home. I want him home with me."

As Mayor Busse tearfully conveyed the final moments of his ordeal, he called on the council to act quickly to take care of the victims' families. He called for a 15-member committee to work on a relief fund of $200,000

Shadows of Chicago

to be extended to the families of the deceased. He also ordered that black and purple drapes be placed on all municipal buildings and that all flags were to be flown at half-staff.[3]

After Busse's pledge to the city council, he would never fully recover from the loss of his childhood friend.[4]

* * * *

Charles Comiskey also took the news of the loss of his old friend very hard. Even though there was never any mention of Comiskey's whereabouts the day of Big Jim's death, the press caught up to him the day after the fire. When reporters asked him questions about his loss, he could barely speak because he was so grief-stricken. Struggling not to break down, he stumbled, "All my life I had known him ...Next to firefighting he loved baseball, and he was one of the best friends the game or the men in it ever had." Once he gathered some strength he said, "He was the most fearless man I have ever known and the squarest as well as the bravest. To me it was like losing a member of my only family. But my loss is nothing compared to what the city of Chicago lost when he went to his death."[5]

Soon after his meeting with reporters, he decided that one game every year at Comiskey Park would be designated as Jim Horan Day. The first game was held on May 26, 1911, and all proceeds from the entire day's events went towards Big Jim's family. For once, Comiskey's nemesis, Ban Johnson, agreed with Comiskey's plan to raise money. Besides Comiskey, the press also interviewed Ban Johnson about the death of his friend. He first told the awful story of how he witnessed rescuers digging "Jim" out from under the rubble. Then he quickly changed the tone of interview by conveying the warm story of the last time he saw him. He proceeded to say that two days prior to his death, when the two were having dinner, Jim was proudly displaying pictures of his kids and telling how important they were to him. Afterward, as the two walked out of the restaurant, Big Jim stopped suddenly in front of a barber shop. He peeked his head in the barbershop and yelled to the barber that he'd see him tomorrow so he could get his hair cut before Christmas. This shows what a unique character he was.[6]

There were many others in the sporting world who offered their pledge to aid the victims' families. Heavyweight boxing champ Jack Johnson proposed that he would he would raise money during his next fight. Jack Johnson added, "I never knew a man with whom I would rather talk fight than Chief Horan. After a fight I showed him how I won a fight by illustrating some of my blows, he came right back and taught me a couple of blows which I intend to use the next time I have a fight."[7]

Besides the sporting world, money flooded in from big businesses around the country, but most would come from area businesses. Even Edward Morris, owner of the Morris Company, who took over a million-dollar hit due to the damage caused by the fire, presented a significant contribution for the victims' families. Perhaps he presented money out of remorse for not helping to install measures that could have saved lives.

* * * *

Despite Morris's negligence, the coroner's jury found that the Morris Company would not be held responsible for the death of the victims. However, they were blamed for numerous inadequate fire prevention measures. The jury cited that each of the warehouses that caught fire, including Warehouse Seven, was not properly ventilated, causing fires to spread quickly throughout the structures. Besides that, it was stated that the Morris buildings had failed numerous electrical inspections due to the chance of arching. An electrical glitch *may* have caused the spark that set off the fire, but due to the fire's overwhelming destruction of Warehouse Seven, it was impossible to make a conclusive investigation into the fire's origin.

The coroner's jury also noted problems with the warehouses' surrounding water system. For one, hydrants were placed so far apart that it required too much manpower to pull the hoses into position—and the greater the feet of hose resulted in the less water pressure. And second, the water mains were incapable of supplying 16-plus engines that were working simultaneously the day of the fire. The investigating city engineer concluded that "the high pressure system in the stockyards would have saved the lives of the brave firemen."

The coroner's jury most urgent recommendation was that the city and the stockyard owners institute Chief Horan's plan for a high-pressure system. And they suggested that the $3,000,000 plan was just pocket change compared to the precious lives and property that would be saved.

But even the jury's recommendation was not enough to introduce the high-pressure system. Instead, the plan was shut down forever by the bureaucratic powers that kept the stockyards running.

However, other recommendations by the jury would trigger the city council to pass ordinances. One such ordinance was that all "buildings of ordinary or mill construction, used for storage and manufacturing purposes and having ground area in excess of 7,500 square feet, of four stories or more in height, shall be equipped with an automatic sprinkler system." Another ordinance required that a sufficient number of fire hydrants be placed throughout the entire stockyard area.[8]

These two reforms would save dozens of firefighters in the years to come, and it would also prevent the hundreds of stockyard fires from ever inciting a citywide disaster again.

---

[1] "Mayor at Horan Bier," *The Daily News,* December 23, 1910.
[2] *Ibid.*
[3] *Ibid.*
[4] "Message of Mayor Sends Victims Aid," *The Daily News,* December 23, 1910.
[5] "Horan Is Praised By Baseball Men," *Chicago Daily Tribune,* December 23, 1910.
[6] Sanborn, I.E., "It Is Provided in the Rules that He Who Heels Also Shall Handle," *Chicago Daily Tribune,* Febuary 18, 1911.
[7] "Horan Is Praised By Baseball Men," *Chicago Daily Tribune,* December 23, 1910.
[8] "Jury To Seek Wire Defects As Cause," *Chicago Examiner,* December 24, 1910, Vol. 9. No. 2.

Shadows of Chicago

Chapter 15

END FOR BUSSE AND THE LEVEE

Up until it was time to run for reelection in early 1911, Mayor Busse was dog-tired of the menacing moral committees, self-righteous politicians, and the ever-hounding general public. He handled their constant demands in the only way he only knew how: as a businessman. Meanwhile, Republican Party supporters who helped him become mayor in the first place were now turning their backs to him because he wasn't willing to play the role of a hardball politician. Instead, they knew, as they always had, that Busse was not the type of person that would aggressively seek his reelection. Not only that, but a few local members of the Republican Party were now under the watchful eye of the Vice Commission, the same committee Busse helped establish. Why would they reward him for being a pain in their side?

Busse could do little but sit back idly to wait to see if his party would nominate him again. All the while, the Republican Party was busy looking for a more bombastic candidate to play political hard-ball against the next Democratic candidate. They thought the best person to accomplish a big win against the Democrats was Charles Merriam, a professor from the University of Chicago and a member of the city council.[1] But Merriam's supposed campaigning prowess proved no match for the veteran politician, Carter Harrison, Jr., who would win the mayor's seat with over 17,000 votes.[2]

On April 17, 1911, the day of Harrison's inauguration as mayor, Busse was expected to present an unfulfilling final message about his four years as mayor, because the city council was accustomed to his swift, monotonous speeches. To the surprise of the city council and the press he provided a lengthy, heartwarming speech about his accomplishments as mayor and how important it was to bring about the reforms he put in place, particularly those that would help curb vice in Chicago. Furthermore, he expressed a number of other issues concerning the city, including fire safety. He said that, "During the year 1910 the fire department responded to more than 12,000 alarms, the largest number in the history of the city. The fire marshal recommends that better fire protection and the high-pressure system should be given immediate consideration, and I endorse this recommendation." He took a quick pause (probably with memories of his friend in mind), and continued to add, "The public is familiar with the appalling loss of life in the stockyards fire of December 22, 1910. The death of the fire marshal and 20 of those who assisted him in fighting the flames should stimulate the interest of citizens and officials in this department to the end that perilous fires may be prevented."[3]

After he offered a few more suggestions that he felt would benefit the city, he exited the city council chambers for the last time. And this time he left with the sound of thankful cheers—and probably a couple jeers.

One of Busse's last public engagements was a little more than one month later, on May 26, 1910, at Comiskey Park. His friend Charlie Comiskey asked that he join him in the grandstands to help him celebrate Jim Horan Day, and also to watch the Sox crush the A's. Yet, Busse's presence in the crowd would be upstaged by the new mayor, Carter Harrison, Jr., who also sat with Comiskey and Busse in the stands. Besides Busse's uneasiness about being in the air of the new mayor, it must have been even more disheartening that he would no longer be watching the game with his old pal, Big Jim.

After Busse disappeared from the political arena, he squandered almost all of his vast wealth he accumulated

Matthew Drew

over the years. Much of it was spent treating his deteriorating health.

On July 9, 1914, after being ill for weeks with heart trouble due to rheumatic attacks, he was sent to Mercy Hospital. As he lay on the hospital bed, surrounded by his wife, Josephine, and his family, he said, "I guess it's pay day for me!" He then took a sip of water that was given to him by his sister and leaned back said, "That's good," and then he died. He passed away from valvular heart disease at only 48-years-old.[4]

According to Norman Mark author of *Mayors, Madams and Madmen*, Busse's widow was left with only 15 cents. However, his personal safe-deposit box was chock-full of stock indicating ownership in a company which sold all the manhole covers to the city.[5] Even though this manhole cover business was a clear ethics violation, it is unclear why his widow could not capitalize on the investment. Instead, she would spend the rest of her life homeless, combing the streets for money.

More ironies continued after Busse's death. Even though Busse was at the forefront of curbing the city's vice district, the newspapers spent little time covering this fact. Actually, newspapers were busy covering the Colosimo/Torrio police murder investigation and the subsequent closing of the Levee.

* * * *

The Vice Commissions Report, titled *Social Evil in Chicago*, was placed on Busse's desk on April 5, 1911, less than two weeks before he was ousted from office, and only once was his name mentioned as facilitator for the report.

Another 30,000 copies of the 368 page report were sent to public officials around the country. Copies of the report were summarized by the nation's newspaper reporters, and then the papers were circulated to just about every literate person in America. Just the basic facts from the report, such as the Chicago's $15,000,000 a year vice market and the 5,000 young women involved in prostitution, were enough to stir outrage. The report also mentioned 52 other American cities, and many of the vice conditions in other cities were found more deplorable than Chicago.

Reporters were required to leave out the specific details of *The Social Evil in Chicago*, and it was even banned from mailings. Some of the details were so shocking they'd be considered X-rated by today's standards. For instance, the report detailed peculiar perversions, the abuse of poor young women, and the staggering amount of drug use. In the Levee alone, four drug stores provided four pounds of morphine and six pounds of cocaine a week to prostitutes. All the while, a number of police officers, politicians, and businessmen, were said to be participants in all the debauchery. But, before any of them could be implicated, a court order was quickly devised to protect corrupt officials.[6]

The Social Evil in Chicago was presented by the Vice Commission to give the public in-your-face facts to stir outrage and to encourage solutions. The report suggested that "constant and persistent repression must be the immediate method; absolute annihilation the ultimate ideal." So, essentially they called for the eradication of the Levee and all other vice districts. They added that this could only come about by constant pressure on the vice district denizens over a long period of years. They suggested that a good way to initiate the Levee raids would be to first finish off the Everleigh Club, which was bringing in hundreds of thousands of dollars per year, by far the most profitable brothel in the Levee.[7]

Finally, the report proposed that a morals commission be formed to provide protection for the thousands of girls involved in prostitution and to help enforce a set of new rules for police to conduct raids on brothels.[8]

* * * *

At the start of Mayor Carter Harrison, Jr.'s term, and months after the Vice Commission report first surfaced, the vice district continued to be a segregated establishment in the First Ward. Harrison did nothing at first, since he inherited former mayor Busses' dilemma: if he didn't do anything about the vice district, he would be ostracized by the general public; if he supported the moral division's raids, he'd make some powerful enemies. He didn't want to make enemies with Hinky-Dink Kenna, Bathhouse Coughlin, or Colosimo—particularly because they all helped Harrison beat Charles Merriam in the polls. Plus, they only helped him to become mayor in the first place, so that he would allow their illegal activities to continue.[9]

Harrison was especially indebted to Hinky-Dink and Bathhouse, since they took the heat for gathering eight drunks from Kenna's Workingman's Exchange to vote twice in his last election—one vote was cast in the First Ward, the second in the Eighteenth. The Hinky-Dink-Bathhouse plan was thwarted by Republican Party members but, amazingly, the infamous duo would still be voted-in as co-aldermen after the First Ward's next election.[10]

Despite his unwillingness to anger the vice element's kingpins, Mayor Harrison had to do something to appease the Vice Commission investigators who continually badgered him. Their primary complaint was that Harrison was doing nothing to shut the doors on the Everleigh Club. He was reluctant to shut down the club, because the Everleigh sisters were paying Coughlin's insurance agency $100 a month, the same fee all the other brothels paid to his agency.[11]

Shadows of Chicago

Soon, though, Harrison would have enough of the Everleigh Club. His blood boiled when the Everleigh sisters designed a booklet containing pictures of the Everleigh Club's décor, the stockyards, and other areas of interest around Chicago. Furthermore, Harrison was mortified when he found out the booklet was circulated around the country and even into Europe. So, upon Harrison's orders on October 25, 1911, at 12:45 in the morning, officers padlocked the doors to the Everleigh Club. As the doors shut for good, Minna Everleigh ordered champagne for all. Then she said stoically, "The ship has sunk... She was a good one. Let's give her a hurrah."[12]

Minna's toast had more symbolic implications than could ever be imagined. For the closing of the Everleigh Club commemorated the beginning of the end for the Levee.

*   *   *   *

As the heat from the morals division fell upon the Levee's brothels, Colosimo moved his office from Colosimos Café to a combination restaurant, saloon, hotel, and brothel at 2001-2003 Archer Avenue. Using protection from a growing number of Italians in the neighborhood, and Hinky-Dink and Bathhouse's associates, his vice realm grew larger than it ever had, even extending beyond city limits. Besides his hidden brothels and gambling dens throughout the city and elsewhere, he controlled more than a hundred businesses, resorts, and opium parlors. At his height as vice lord, he was bringing in a half-million dollars a year.[13]

Colosimo's second-in-command, Johnny Torrio, provided him with so much loyal service that he gave Torrio the okay to command his own criminal organization. Torrio first ran his criminal network out of the Four Deuces, a four-story building at 2222 South Wabash. Torrio had a legitimate saloon on the first floor, gambling dens on the second and the third, and a brothel on the fourth floor to hide from the growing police presence. And like Colosimo, his criminal empire would soon spread throughout the city and into the suburbs. To protect his growing enterprise he paid off his own police and politicians and corralled his own group of thugs he knew from his James Street gang in New York.[14]

The most infamous hoodlum Torrio fetched from New York was Alphonse "Scarface" Capone. Capone had no problem coming to Chicago to help his former boss and the godfather to his son, Albert Francis "Sonny" Capone. On top of helping Torrio, the move to Chicago couldn't have come at a better time. At the same time, Capone was in hiding for beating an Irishman, Arthur Finnegan, to death—a strong-arm for a powerful crime leader, William Lovett. As a result, in Chicago, Capone assumed the name Al Brown, and took on a $15-a-week mop-boy job at Torrio's Four Deuces. At the Deuces, he would soon move up to "capper," a job that called for him to stand outside, hollering for people to come inside.[15] Right away his enormous presence scared the pants off of any passerby—wallets included. But, for the time being, Capone would have to watch and learn from the Colosimo and Torrio outfits, before he'd finagle his way to the top.

In 1911, Colosimo's and Torrio's smooth-sailing criminal networks would hit some stormy weather. New difficulties came from agents from the Bureau of Investigation of the U.S. Justice Department (later named the FBI). The Justice Department was tipped off by a prostitute in Connecticut who said that she was transferred past state lines for immoral purposes by Colosimo, Torrio, and Van Bever—a clear violation of the Mann Act. Her testimony would surely place them in the slammer if they didn't do something to intervene. Before the girl was about to testify, two men claiming to be federal agents nabbed her, and a day later her lifeless body was found with 12 bullet holes. Because the star witness was no longer able to testify against Colosimo, Torrio, and Van Bever, the justice department had no other choice but to set them free.[16]

More heat came in 1914. This time pressure came from the Morals Division, a newly formed branch of the Chicago Police Department. The new members of the Morals Division worked as a separate unit that did not have to answer to corrupt political and police officials, so they were off the Colosimo, Torrio, and hinky-Dink/Bathhouse payrolls. So, it was apparent to all that a raid on every Levee establishment was imminent. This prompted Colosimo to hold a meeting at his café for all Levee bosses to attend. The objective was to find a way to knock off the Morals Division officers before their vice businesses were shut down.[17]

On July 16, 1914, the Morals Division officers implemented their raid on Levee bosses. Meanwhile, acting on tip, Colosimo had already prepared to go to war that day. To defend the Levee he called on his second in command, Torrio, to find a way to gun down the Morals Division officers. For extra muscle, Torrio called on his cousin, Rocco "Roxy" Vanille, from New York.

When the arresting officers entered the Levee with their paddy wagons and started to arrest three women and one man, a crowd of screaming spectators greeted them, yelling all kinds of obscenities. Behind the crowd was a red sedan that crept slowly, driven by "The Fox" Torrio. His two passengers were his cousin Roxy and one of Colosimo's thugs, Mac Fitzpatrick.

At 9:35 p.m., two plain-clothes detectives, Merrill and Amort, were at 22nd and Wabash when a brick was thrown in their direction by a big, dark-haired man in a light gray suit. One of the two officers drew his gun and pointed it in the direction of the mysterious man and several hecklers. Seconds later, the man in the light gray suit stepped out from behind a woman and began firing at the two officers. One bullet hit Detective Merrill in the leg.

Hearing the sounds of gunfire, another two plainclothes officers, Sgt. Stanley J. Birns and his partner, Detective John C. Sloop, ran in the direction of the ruckus with their pistols drawn.[18] Supposedly, neither Birns nor Sloop knew that Merrill and Amort were cops, so they began firing at them. The oncoming bullets caused Merrill and Amort to dart behind a doorway for cover and proceed to return fire. During the melee, Sgt. Birns was stuck in the shoulder and abdomen and flopped flat onto to the cobblestone street.

In the midst of the bizarre gun battle, a uniformed officer nearby came upon a wounded man who had been shot in the foot. The officer let him go, assuming he was an innocent bystander. The fact was that the wounded man was later found to be Roxy Vanille, and it was Torrio who then helped him get back into his red sedan.

After the shooting stopped, Sgt. Birns was dragged to an ambulance and brought to the hospital, where he would die. During the autopsy, there were two bullets removed from his body, both .22 caliber specials, the type used by all members of the police department, which indicated that he fell victim to friendly fire. However, another bullet pulled from a wounded spectator was not the type of bullet issued to the police officers.[19]

This provoked investigators to place blame for the officer's death on the mysterious "man in gray," who they determined instigated the gun battle. Soon they surmised from numerous eye-witness accounts of the incident that the unknown assailant was Roxy Vanille. After Vanille was treated for his shattered ankle from the gunshot, he was placed in jail to await sentencing for murder. And since Torrio drove the getaway car, he was indicted for conspiracy. But he would skip town before his arraignment. Colosimo, on the other hand, was arrested and placed in jail for conspiracy to obstruct justice for planning to hide

Shadows of Chicago

Vanille and Torrio. This would be first time Colosimo was arrested and placed in prison.[20]

As an added insult, Mayor Harrison ordered the police to close down Colosimo's Café. Soon after, by the end of 1914, the last of the brothels were raided. Open prostitution in the Levee was no more.

* * * *

Gangster James "Big Jim" Colosimo with attorney Charles Erbstein following his first arrest; 1914 Photographer--Chicago Daily News, Inc. Chicago History Museum, #DN-0063234.

Jim Colosimo would only see a half-day in jail. This was all the time it took for the judge to release him on $5,000 bond. The only charge against him was for operating the Colosimo Café beyond the 1:00 a.m. closing. The state's attorney had nothing with which to convict him for his involvement in Sgt. Birns's death, and they never would. With the help of Hinky-Dink's and Bathhouse's influence on the judicial system, all the suspects in the criminal investigation were let go due to misinformation from witnesses. Right away, Colosimo resumed his criminal network, and Johnny Torrio would come out of hiding to rejoin his uncle.[21]

On top of beating the wrap, Mayor Harrison, in an effort to restore peace with his former supporters, Hinky-Dink, Bathhouse, and Colosimo, reissued the liquor license for the his Colosimo's Café. In addition, Harrison decided not to seek his reelection the following year, opening the way for them to support a new mayoral candidate who would allow their vice operations to continue.

Although Hinky-Dink, Bathhouse, and Colosimo almost always supported Democratic candidates, they chose to change their support for a Republican this time, Alderman William "Big Bill" Thompson. Thompson came from an aristocratic family in Boston. Instead of accepting to live a life similar to his prominent family members, he entertained his dream of being a cowboy for a living. At 15, he traveled to Wyoming to herd cattle, tame wild horses, and work on a variety of ranches.[22] When he came to Chicago, the six-foot-tall Thompson became a Levee regular, and amassed such a unique reputation that people around him suggested he enter politics. Soon after, he joined the Republican Party and quickly assumed the position of Second Ward alderman.

With the combined help of Colosimo, Hinky-Dink and Bathhouse, he would easily win the mayoral election, and would eventually become the most crooked mayor in Chicago history. Immediately upon taking office, he repaid his vice element supporters by dismantling the Morals Division on the police department. He first achieved this goal by replacing top members of the division with associates who would have to answer to him. With the

Shadows of Chicago

Morals Division in disarray, Hinky Dink's and Bathhouse's liquor establishments continued unabated as they had been prior to the raids on Levee. This also allowed the Colosimo/Torrio criminal enterprise to once again flourish within the city boundaries.

Colosimo, now with Mayor Thompson as his ally, functioned as a new person. Surprisingly to all, he started to act more and more like celebrity, and less like the fearsome vice lord he was before. For instance, instead of spending the majority of his time running his criminal syndicate from the backroom of Colosimo's Café, he began spending more time in the restaurant section and his casino, gallivanting with the upper-class socialites. When he wasn't rubbing elbows with local celebrities, he was out traveling around the country and in Europe, gambling, drinking, and enjoying everything life had to offer.

Then, one day at his café, he saw a woman who would change his life forever. In the midst of hobnobbing with guests in the restaurant, his attention was snatched by a beautiful, talented young woman singing on stage. Her name was Dale Winters, a 19-year old-girl from Ohio who was using her singing talents to buy her mother a new house. Every time she took the stage, the angelic looking brunette was constantly bombarded by suitors afterwards. Like so many men who tried to woo her, Colosimo went to make his move. Even though Dale was nearly half his age and he was married, he began taking her out to the finest restaurants around town, buying her fine jewelry and clothes, and even provided her with the best voice coach that money could buy.

Meanwhile, noticing Colosimo in a stupor, Torrio warned him about his new love interest. Ironically, Torrio, a Roman Catholic (obviously not a practicing one), advised that Colosimo end his relationship with Dale because it wasn't appropriate. Upon his warning, Colosimo refused to end his affair. At that, Torrio snapped, "Well, it's your funeral." Weeks after, instead of heading Torrio's threat, Colosimo left his wife, Victoria, and married his new sweetheart, Dale Winters.[23]

It wasn't just Colosimo's new relationship that bothered Torrio. It was also the fact that his relationship, as well as new celebrity status, had made him neglect his duties as vice lord. Torrio, more than ever before, needed Colosimo's backing, because the 18th Amendment, or Prohibition Act, had just passed, and the Chicago outfit needed to keep the liquor flowing without police interference. At first, despite police raids going on throughout the city and suburbs, Torrio and Colosimo worked together with their network of bootleggers to provide booze to the Levee and the south and west suburbs by paying off police and deputy sheriffs. In a surprise move, a short time later, Colosimo surrendered the bootlegging business to Torrio and his rising associate Al Capone, so he could focus on his new wife and the affairs of the café. Ultimately, his rash decision caused him to lose prominence in the outfit, and also made him a target.

A week after his marriage, on May 11, 1920, Colosimo received a phone call from Torrio, telling him to report to his office to pick up a shipment of whiskey at his café. At first he refused, until Torrio convinced him to go there in person. Once he arrived at the café, he walked through the dining room to his office. Once there, he asked his bookkeeper Frank Camilla and his chef if anyone had called, and then he walked over to the office lobby. A moment later, the bookkeeper and the chef heard two blaring gunshots. As they entered the lobby to see where the sounds were coming from, to their horror, they found Colosimo lying on the vestibule tile floor in a thick pool of blood. He would die minutes later from a one-bullet wound that penetrated his brain through an entry would in back of his ear, another bullet was buried in the wall nearby.[24]

Shadows of Chicago

At his funeral he had 53 pall-bearers, a few of them judges and congressmen—one of which was Bathhouse John Coughlin. On top of that, there were a thousand First Ward Democrats and 4,000 other mourners marching his body towards Oakwood cemetery, where he was buried. Since he was denied a Catholic burial, because he was divorced, Bathhouse said a prayer next to Colosimo's grave.[25] After his prayer, Torrio, who fronted the money for the entire funeral, spoke on his uncle's behalf. At one point, he said, "Big Jim and me, we're like brothers."[26]

Not surprisingly, after an inconclusive murder investigation by police, all fingers pointed to Torrio as being the one who called the hit. Although it was never proven, he had the most to gain from the murder for a number of reasons. He wanted to take over Colisimo's entire criminal network, he had bribed just about every local police officer, and he had dozens of unidentifiable New York thugs to make the hit possible. The question was then, who was the most likely candidate contracted out to kill Colosimo? The likeliest killer would have to be the one who one of the witnesses described as a heavy-set man with scars on the left side of his face. These specific details reduced all other suspects down to one—Al Capone.[27] Plus, Al Capone when asked years later about the murder, said, "Colosimo had a lot of money" and "Johnny wanted a big cut." He also added that Torrio thought he was "growing soft."[28]

Whether or not Johnny "The Fox" Torrio did the deed, he became top member of the Chicago outfit. His leadership would take hold during the most notorious era in history, the Prohibition. During these years, Chicago became the leader in unsolved murders.

---

[1] Flanagan, Maureen A. "Fred Busse: A Silent Mayor in Turbulent Times." *The Mayors: the Chicago Political Tradition.* Carbondale: Southern Illinois University Press, 1995.

[2] Harrison served two consecutive terms as mayor (1897-1905). And then another four year term after Fred Busse (1911-1915).
[3] "Exit Mayor Busse: Enter Mayor Harrison," *Chicago Daily Tribune,* April 18, 1911.
[4] "Death Closes Varied Career of Fred Busse," *Chicago Daily Tribune,* July 10, 1914.
[5] Johnson, Curt. *Wicked City. Chicago: From Kenna to Capone.* December Press. 1994.
[6] *Ibid.*
[7] "5,000 Souls and 15,000,000 a Year Tribute To Vice," *Chicago Daily Tribune,* April 6, 1911.
[8] Keating, Ann Durkin, et al., *The Encylopedia of Chicago*, Chicago: The University of Chicago Press.
[9] Bilek, Arthur J. *The First Vice Lord: Big Jim Colosimo and the Ladies of the Levee.* Nashville: Cumberland House Publishing, 2008.
[10] *Ibid.*
[11] *Ibid.*
[12] Johnson.
[13] Bilek.
[14] Russo, Gus. *The Outfit: The Role of Chicago's Underworld in the Shaping of Modern America.* Bloomsbury. New York, N.Y.
[15] *Ibid.*
[16] *Ibid.*
[17] Bilek.
[18] Later it was found that Sloop was an agent of one of the Levee bosses.
[19] Bilek.
[20] *Ibid.*
[21] *Ibid.*
[22] *Ibid.*
[23] *Ibid.*
[24] *Ibid.*
[25] Johnson.
[26] Bilek.
[27] Russo.
[28] Bilek.

Shadows of Chicago

Chapter 16

THE BLACK SOX

Charles Comiskey achieved the impossible. His 1917 team was the best team he ever beheld. This was due, for the most part, because he travelled to just about every corner of the nation to hand-pick the best ball players for his White Sox, while less aggressive team owners typically focused on signing easy-to-reach players who derived from their particular team's neck-of-the-woods. Plus, compared to other club owners, he was willing to spend more money on his players' salaries. Comiskey's assertive signing skills would bring some of the best, and some of the wiliest players, to the White Sox.

The 1917 pitching staff produced the lowest ERA in the league and the second-least runs allowed. The biggest stand-out pitchers were Urban "Red" Faber, Claude "Lefty" Williams, and Eddie Cicotte. Red Faber, the spit-baller (it was legal then), had an unimpressive 1917 season—but he was a great closer and even greater pitcher in the clutch. Lefty Williams was a better pitcher than Faber, with a 17-8 record in 1917, but rarely came through for the team when his skills were most needed. The most controversial of the three, Eddie Cicotte, was signed by Comiskey on July 10, 1912. The 28-year-old Eddie Cicotte was signed for his impressive throwing arm, and he was not getting along with the Red Sox manager. In fact, he didn't get along with anyone. In particular, many opposing players disliked him because he was known to throw "shine ball." The "shine ball" was an illegal method of applying slick substances to baseballs so they would zig-zag towards the plate, causing batters to misread the balls' trajectory and whiff-out.

Shadows of Chicago

The 1917 World Series champs Chicago White Sox posing in front of the grandstands at Comiskey Park (eight of players would be found guilty of throwing the 1919 World Series); 1917; Photographer--Chicago Daily News. Chicago History Museum, #SDN-010040.

Despite his troubled reputation, Comiskey must have known that Cicotte would turn out to be a formidable White Sox pitcher. In the 1917 season, he had the team's most wins (28), most strikeouts (150), and the lowest ERA (1.53).

One of the reasons the pitchers' ERAs were the lowest in the league were also due to excellent fielding. Two of Comiskey's brightest stars on defense were the Collins' "brothers," Eddie and Shano. Although not related, the two seemed inseparable due to their combined fielding and hitting skills. Shano had a wicked right fielder's arm, was a master at hitting triples with loaded bases, and had an uncanny ability to come through in the clutch.

His "brother" Eddie was the best second basemen the Sox ever had, and in 1917 hit .289 with 91 runs batted in. For many seasons his impressive hitting skills were only outmatched by Detroit's Ty Cobb in the AL batting race. But as far as natural hitting ability was concerned, "Shoeless" Joe Jackson should have taken the crown over both Collinses and Cobb.[1]

Before Shoeless Joe came to the Sox, he had a .371 batting average. Comiskey was able to purchase the 26-year-old in 1915, because the Cleveland Indians' owner, Charles Somers, could not pay him the salary he wanted. So, Comiskey was able to strike a deal that would cost him $31,500, three players, and required him to sign a three-year deal with Jackson—but it all seemed to be worth it. In the 1917 season, Shoeless Joe proved to be a solid left fielder and a game-winning batter, hitting .301, with 91 runs-batted-in, and the team's highest slugging percentage, .429. The only player on the team who had a higher batting average that year was Oscar "Happy" Felsch. The 22-year-old center fielder was quick as a wink and was expected to remain atop the hitting leader's board for years to come.[2]

For Comiskey there were only two puzzle pieces missing to make the 1917 season perfect: a first basemen and a shortstop. As the team entered the 1917 season, the dynamic puzzle was completed by the purchase of Chick Gandil from Cleveland and Charles "Swede" Risberg, an average hitter but incredible infielder, from the Pacific Coast League. In the 1917 season, the two talented prospects had a less than spectacular year. Actually, Gandil's most memorable game was when he fist-fought a Red Sox player in the White Sox dugout. And Gandil's equally troubled partner, Risberg, became the only player in history to be taken out of the World Series lineup because he complained too much about a boil that bothered him. It's hard to believe this infamous duo would be the driving force that would one day divide the White Sox team in two.[3]

Despite the wide array of characters on the 1917 roster, they were the best team Comiskey had ever assembled. At the beginning of the season, however, the players had something new to be concerned about. The season began a week after the U.S. entered World War I, and almost all of his players could be called to support the war effort. To help the team accept the inevitable, Comiskey's ordered them to register for the military draft on May 23 at the Chicago City Clerk's office, so they would all be registered before the June 5 deadline—the same day as their road game in Philadelphia.[4]

After a series of wins on the road, the White Sox looked like a team destined to win the pennant. During one of their outings at Boston's Fenway Park, when the White Sox were winning 2-0, and the rain began to fall in the fifth inning, a crowd stormed onto the field to try to delay the game long enough for a postponement. To the crowd's dismay, the game continued and the White Sox won 7-2. It was found later that the crowd members were all gamblers who had bet heavily on a Red Sox win. The game signified what was happening at ballparks around the nation, for in every major stadium gamblers were "influencing" many of the games' outcomes, and there was little to prevent them from doing so. Even the smartest owners, like Comiskey, could do little but hope that their players were not ones throwing games on the gambler's dime.[5]

As rumors of fixes abounded, Comiskey trained his focus on his team's quest for the World Series. On September 21, the White Sox clinched the American League pennant with a 2-1 win over the Red Sox, and eight days later they pulled out their 100th win against the Yankees, a first for the White Sox. But the team's biggest challenge was yet to come. They were about to face the powerhouse of the NL, the New York Giants, for the best of seven games in the

World Series. The Giants were a 98-56 team, and won the NL pennant by 10 games.[6]

In anticipation of the World Series, Comiskey inflated the stadium by 32,000 seats. Every seat was filled for the 2-1 win over the Giants in the first game. The win was attributed to Happy Felsch's homer in the fourth inning.

The most thrilling Sox win was during a 2-2 tie-breaker game. The Giants were ahead 5-2 after six innings, when the Sox scored three runs in the seventh inning, and then another three in the eighth. The amazing comeback win was due to the 3-4-5 hitters, Eddie Collins, Shoeless Joe, and Happy Felsch. The sensational three were also in charge of taking the series the following game in New York. However, the 4-2 series ender was not without controversy. In the fourth inning on a weak grounder hit by Eddie Collins, the Giants' third basemen, Heinie Zimmerman, threw an uncharacteristically wild throw over the first baseman's head. With Collins now on second base, Shoeless Joe hit a can-of-corn pop-fly to the right fielder. The ball was dropped, sending Collins to third and Shoeless Joe to second. The next Sox batter, Felsch, hit a grounder to the pitcher, putting Collins in an impossible run-down between third and home. For some reason, Zimmerman, the third baseman, was strangely protecting home plate instead of third and missed an easy tag, sending Collins in for the first run of the game. Zimmerman's foul-up was so theatrical-looking that details of the play made it into all the nation's papers the following day. Instead of giving up on his acting career, Zimmerman got busted trying to fix another game in 1919, banishing him from baseball forever.

Neglecting the fact that certain details of the series win seemed unusual, Comiskey was happy with victory over the Giants. But, as always, he thirsted for more. Not only did he want to dominate the major leagues for as long as possible, he also wanted to continue expanding baseball's popularity throughout the world.[7]

For the time being he needed to concentrate on continuing the Sox dynasty into the 1918 season. His effort to make this happen was complicated by his star players being called for military service throughout the season. A few players were called for active duty, while others like Shoeless Joe, Lefty Williams, and Happy Felsch avoided active service by working in the war-related industry (shipbuilding, mostly). The "draft-dodgers," as Comiskey called them, enraged him so much he vowed that they'd never be allowed to return to the White Sox. By the beginning of the 1919 season, however, every one of the so-called "draft-dodgers" was brought back to the team—but most would still harbor animosity towards Comiskey for his rash decision. In Comiskey's defense, he was an avid supporter of the American cause in the Big War.[8]

The unusual circumstances surrounding the 1918 season, along with Cicotte's sore shoulder (he went 12-19), caused the World Series champs to finish in sixth place by the end of the season. Other teams in the league also lost players to the war effort and team revenues dropped nationwide. So, at the beginning of the 1918-1919 off-season, owners, in preparation for the ongoing Big War, decided to shorten the 1919 season, and some considered cancelling the 1919 season altogether. To everyone's surprise the war ended by November 1918 and owners again expected to regain high-attendance levels.

Comiskey saw the 1919 season as a chance to regain the top-notch caliber they had in 1917 and again win the World Series. Besides, the line-up was the same, and as an added bonus he signed Kid Gleason, the best manager Comiskey believed would thrust the team in the direction of the pennant.

Whether Gleason had something to do with it or not, the Sox began the season with some fine hitting by Shoeless

Joe, Happy Felsch, and Eddie Collins, accompanied by some solid pitching by Lefty Williams and Eddie Cicotte. Due to the team's combined skills up until the end of May, the Sox had a 27-7 record and a five-game lead in the AL. But the beginning season romp was interrupted by Chick Gandil's fight with Tris Speaker of the Cleveland Indians during a game at Comiskey Park. After Gandil accused Speaker of "spiking him" with his shoes during a slide, the two players delivered connecting head-snapping blows for three minutes until they were separated by umpires and managers.[9]

After the fight, coincidently or not, the Sox entered June on a downslide, and quickly fell out of first by the middle of the month. June proved to be a month of gloom—for a number of reasons. For one, players' stats declined because there was growing tension in the Sox dugout as opposing cliques began to form. Second, at the beginning of June, Comiskey, with the help of local police, began to bust up a growing number of gamblers in the stadium, resulting in several arrests. Third, beer sales ended at Comiskey Park, due to a new prohibition law in the state of Illinois. This certainly infuriated the best of fans.[10]

The White Sox caught their second wind by mid-July, remaining in first in the AL for the remainder of the regular season. The Sox's domination over the AL teams could not have happened without the outstanding pitching of Eddie Cicotte. His accomplishments included a 29-7 record, a .806 winning percentage, five shut-outs, and an ERA of 1.82. His regular season stats would have been more impressive if he wasn't taken out of the lineup for two weeks on September 5, due to a sore shoulder—the same injury plagued him much of his career. But this time, the injury proved to be too much for him. He was also 35-years-old, set to retire, and he hated Comiskey. All these realities influenced his decision to consider an offer from sport's gamblers.

Shadows of Chicago

In the 1919 season, while Cicotte led the team in pitching, Shoeless Joe led the team in hitting. He was the club leader in five categories: batting average (.351), on-base percentage (.422), slugging percentage (.506), homeruns (tied at 7), and runs-batted-in (96). The other players to reach the club leader board were Happy Felsch, Lefty Williams, and Eddie Collins. Only one of six club leaders would *not* strike a deal with sport's gamblers.[11]

The 1919 White Sox easily took the American League pennant on September 24, with a 6-5 victory over the Browns at Comiskey Park. On the National League side, the Cincinnati Reds clinched the pennant, their first since 1882. As word came that Reds would be going to the World Series, everyone decided that they would be the clear underdogs.[12] The Reds were considered a group of average players, nothing compared to big-name, series-winning players on the White Sox. Not only that, but the AL dominated the decade so far, winning eight of the nine World Series titles. This drove the gambling stakes in the Sox's favor through the roof.

But gamblers had already foreseen a lopsided World Series. In fact, before either the White Sox or the Reds took their respective pennants, gamblers were already preparing a fix. Two days after the Reds won their pennant, and six days before the Sox won theirs, on September 18, big-time bookmaker Joseph "Sport" Sullivan met with Chick Gandil to discuss details of the fix. Gandil proceeded to tell Sullivan that he would gather enough Sox players to throw the series. In return, Sullivan agreed to give the willing participants a total of $80,000.

On the following day, September 19, after a 3-2 win against the Red Sox in Boston, Gandil approached Swede Risberg, Cicotte, and Lefty Williams about the details. Seconds later, Cicotte said he required $10,000 up front. Meanwhile, an eavesdropping Fred McMullin demanded that he be included. Next, Lefty Williams expressed his dissatisfaction, and then he changed his mind once he realized that the fix would go on without him.

The day after, on September 20, all eight of the infamous Black Sox players convened for the first time. Chick Gandil, Eddie Cicotte, Happy Felsch, Shoeless Joe Jackson, Fred McMullin, Swede Risberg, Buck Weaver, and Lefty Williams met at the Hotel Ansonia in New York to discuss the offer Sport Sullivan was about to present to them. Supposedly, Sullivan presented seven of the players an undisclosed sum that was more than most of the players made during the 1919 season. Weaver, despite witnessing the money changing hands, never took a dime.[13]

After the Hotel Ansonia meeting, Gandil and Cicotte took control of the rest of the arrangement. They tried to finagle a deal with Sullivan, and another bankroller, ex-Sox player Bill Burns, for an additional $100,000 to be paid to the players before the World Series. But, neither Sullivan nor Burns could bankroll that kind of dough, so they called on Arnold Rothstein, the most notorious sports gambler, known as "The Big Bankroll." At first Rothstein refused, but then reconsidered, in part, because he had good ties with Sullivan.[14]

Before Rothstein fronted the money, he did a little research to make sure the Black Sox wouldn't renege on their promises to throw the Series. Then, believing that the fix would pan out, he planned to wire Sullivan $40,000 to spread out to the players, and another $40,000 would be placed in a safe at the Congress Hotel to be distributed to the players once the Sox lost the series. As added insurance on the transaction, Rothstein required that Cicotte hit the leadoff Cincinnati batter in the first game of the Series.

A half-hour before the first game of the World Series at Red Stadium, manager Kid Gleason, during the pre-game pep-talk, spoke about rumors of a fix. As he focused his accusing glares on a number of players, some looked visually shocked, and others pointed their heads towards

Shadows of Chicago

the ground. At this point, Shoeless Joe asked Gleason to be taken out of the game because he was ill—probably sickened by thought of letting down his team. Gleason refused his request and ordered him to play the game.[15]

Sure enough, in the bottom of the first inning, Cicotte pelted the Red's leadoff batter, signaling to the Black Sox and the bookies that the fix was on. Cicotte stayed in game until he was yanked out in the bottom of the fourth for giving up five runs. Right after the Sox's 9-1 loss, Kid Gleason approached Cicotte after the game in a hotel lobby and openly accused him of throwing the game. It wasn't revealed how Cicotte responded to the accusations, but later that evening, Gleason met with Comiskey to discuss the obvious fix. Comiskey reacted by contacting AL president Ban Johnson. Johnson, rarely taking Comiskey seriously, accused him of being a sore loser.5 When equally suspicious journalists approached Johnson, he responded that Comiskey's suspicions were "the yelp of a beaten cur," and that there wasn't a chance that all the players could be involved in a fix.[16]

After the first game of the series, a number of Black Sox players were eager to receive their compensation. To their dismay, instead of paying-out the $40,000 promised to them, Sullivan had used $29,000 to bet on the Reds. Instead, he presented Gandil with $10,000. Gandil was livid, but ran with the money anyway, and then hid it under Cicotte's pillow. Soon after, Cicotte, equally irate, proceeded to sew the money into the lining of his jacket.[17]

On top of that, Abe Atell, Rothstein's ex-boxer sidekick, informed the Black Sox players that they would now receive $20,000 after every loss and were required to lose the first three games. By this time, most of the players wanted out, but they were already neck-deep in mud, so they felt they had no choice but to accept Atell's proposal and continue throw game two of the series.

During game two, Lefty Williams was on the mound, throwing an unusual amount of wild pitches. And any time the catcher, Ray Schalk, signaled for him to throw a pitch that was certain strike out batters, Williams would wave him off and proceed to throw a meatball towards the plate. Due to his less-than-average pitching, the Reds scored three runs in the fourth inning that proved to be the game-ender. Before the Sox lost 4-2 in the seventh inning at Cinci, an ironic occurrence happened. A stuffed dummy dropped from the sky and landed in the middle of the field, apparently the result of a practical joker throwing it from an airplane.

The dummy was not the only one dropped to the ground that day. After the game, Ray Schalk pummeled Lefty Williams for throwing the game. Also, at the same time, but in a separate incident, manager Kid Gleason clocked-out Chick Gandil (the ex-boxer) for his apparent leadership role in the fix. A day after the beat-down and still nursing his injuries, Gandil approached bankrollers Bill Burns and Billy Maharg and told them to bet all their dirty money on the Reds. Amusingly, doing as Gandil suggested, they became appalled when the White Sox shutout the Reds 3-0 the following game—two of runs came from Gandil's single in the second inning—costing the gamblers a fortune.[18]

Gandil's game-changing hit concerned Sullivan as well. On top of that, Gandil told Sullivan that he wanted out of the fix. At that, Sullivan offered Gandil $20,000 before game four, and another $40,000 before game five. Accepting the new offer, Gandil dished out $5,000 each to Happy Felsch, Shoeless Joe, Swede Risberg, and Lefty Williams to keep the fix alive.

After the new offer, in game four the White Sox again fell to the Reds 2-0, giving the Reds a 3-1 lead in the series. The Reds won on two errors by Cicotte: one was a wild throw past the first baseman, and another was a dropped ball that allowed a runner to stretch a single.[19]

The fix continued into game five with a 5-0 loss at Comiskey Park. This time the game was botched by Lefty Williams's poor pitching in the six inning (four runs were given up), and Happy Felsch's costly misplay in center field. After the game, Sullivan again failed to pay the Black Sox the $20,000 they anticipated. Not surprising, Sullivan knew that he no longer needed the players to throw games, since the White Sox were down 4-1 in the best of nine series. Knowing that the White Sox needed to win all their remaining games if they wanted to win the Series, they turned up the heat, winning the next two games due to excellent hitting by Buck Weaver, Shoeless Joe, Chick Gandil, and Shano Collins. Even Eddie Cicotte pitched an outstanding game-winner in game seven.[20]

Despite the team's impressive effort on the comeback trail, on October 9, in front of 32,930 excited fans at Comiskey Park, the White Sox lost the World Series. The final loss was due to the Reds' four-run first-inning romp off of Lefty Williams. According to Williams later, he purposely let up the runs because gamblers threatened to physically harm him and his wife if he didn't fix the game. Even though the threat may have occurred, it was still his third loss of the series.[21]

Once the series ended, Sport Sullivan retrieved the $40,000 from the safe at the Congress Hotel, brought the money to Gandil's room, then gave $10,000 to Swede Risberg, $5,000 to Fred McMullin, and the rest to Gandil. When all was said and done, of the $80,000 promised, $35,000 went to Chick Gandil, $15,000 to Swede Risberg, $10,000 to Eddie Cicotte, and only $5,000 went to Shoeless Joe Jackson, Lefty Williams, Happy Felsch and Fred McMullin each.

Matthew Drew

After the last dollar was paid to the players after the series, the moment marked the beginning of the horror that would befall the infamous Black Sox.

* * * *

Shoeless Joe sat nervously outside of Comiskey's office. With him, he had his $5,000 in his pocket, and a boatload of guilt he was prepared to spill out. It was a day after the final game of the World Series, and hopefully his owner would take all the money, so he could relieve some of the burning guilt bothering him since he decided to be in on the fix.[22] To his dismay, he sat outside of his office for several hours, and, allegedly, before he walked away, he left a note that stated he would reveal everything about the fix. Meanwhile, Comiskey sat alone in office, contemplating a way to approach the press that day.

Comiskey knew the fix was larger and more complicated than he could ever imagine. Plus, facts about the most infamous baseball scandal in history would prove to be too much for his fans to bear. Knowing this, he had to proceed cautiously as he dealt with the press. On October 10, when press questioned him about the allegations, he truthfully answered that he didn't know the extent of the details of the fix, but offered a $20,000 reward for anyone with information to come forward.

For months after the series, Comiskey was torn. He wanted to protect the image of his ball club, but he didn't want the players who threw the series to get away with it. Regardless, talk of the scandal would not go away, yet the general public was still unaware of what was going on. On December 15, 1919, Hugh Fullerton, writer for *New York World*, suggested that the World Series was fixed and that owners did little to intervene while the outcomes of games were being bought and sold. The fact was, however, that baseball owners, like Comiskey, had their arms tied behind

Shadows of Chicago

their backs. They were not omniscient and couldn't possibly know every fix that went on behind closed doors. Besides that, for Comiskey and other owners, it could be damaging to their ball clubs to speculate on players' involvement with sports gamblers. In Comiskey's case, the only solid evidence about the World Series fix was that Gandil purchased a new automobile and diamonds, and Cicotte recently paid off the mortgage on his farm.[23]

So, with little evidence to go on, on December 19, Comiskey told the press, "We have been investigating all the rumors and I have had men working 24 hours a day running down clues that promised to produce the facts. Nothing came of them. Do not get the impression that I am through investigating." Comiskey added, "If I land the goods on any of my ballplayers I will see that there is no place in organized ball for them."[24]

Comiskey had little choice but to begin the following season under a cloud of suspicion for his team's involvement in throwing the series. Of the eight Black Sox, only one, Chick Gandil, never returned to the roster. Gandil took his payout and ran, hoping to never come back. Without Gandil the team played at pre-World Series caliber, storming into 1920 with impressive wins and bringing in record-level attendance. Actually, the team's hitting was better than ever. The combined hitting of Shoeless Joe, Eddie Collins, and Buck Weaver still reign as the three highest single-season numbers in White Sox history. But, as the team played at levels that made them shoo-ins for the AL pennant, there were rumors in dugout that they were all about to be called in to testify about their knowledge of the 1919 fix.[25]

On September 21, 1920, it was official. The Assistant State's Attorney announced that players, owners, managers, and gamblers would testify before the grand jury.

Comiskey was the first to testify. In front of the grand jury he said, "If any of my players are not honest, I'll fire them no matter who they are, and if I can't get honest players to fill their places, I'll close the gates of the park that I have spent a lifetime to build and in which, in the declining years of my life, I take the greatest measure of pride."[26]

Comiskey would get his chance to rid the team of the Black Sox players. This came after Cicotte admitted to the grand jury that he accepted $10,000 dollars to throw the game. Soon after, Shoeless Joe testified that he took $5,000 of the $20,000 he was promised, and he implicated Gandil and Risberg. Cicotte's and Shoeless Joe's testimonies prompted Lefty Williams and Happy Felsch to turn themselves in. Finally, the names of the eight Black Sox players were exposed to the public for the first time: Gandil, Cicotte, Jackson, Risberg, Weaver, Felsch, Williams, and McMullin. As soon as Comiskey heard the news, he immediately suspended the players. He said, "[I]t is due to the public that I take this action even though it costs Chicago the pennant."[27]

Two days after Comiskey's comment, the Indians clinched the AL pennant over the remaining players not implicated in the scandal. Feeling sorry for the players not on the take, Comiskey sent them all a check for $1,500, and said they should be compensated for having to suffer through the scandal.

On October 22, the eight Black Sox were formerly indicted for fixing the series, along with Arnold Rothstein and Abe Atell, Bill Burns, Sport Sullivan, Nat Evans, and former White Sox pitcher Hal Chase, on nine counts of conspiracy.[28] The case went to trial on July 19, 1921.

Front page headlines from around the country announced the trial against the eight Black Sox and the gamblers. After deliberating for two hours, the jury came back with a not guilty verdict for all the defendants, due to insufficient evidence. The acquittal sent a rush of cheers through the courtroom, and then the eight Black Sox went over to thank each of the jurors.[29]

The following morning, the Black Sox celebration was cut short by Judge Kenesaw Mountain Landis. Landis, the newly assigned baseball commissioner, had a reputation of being a righteous judge and an avid supporter of clean baseball, and would prove to be not as merciful as the trial's judge. To the press he stated, "Regardless of the verdict of juries, no player who throws a ballgame, no player that undertakes or promises to throw a ballgame, no player who sits in conference with a bunch of crooked players and gamblers where the ways and means of throwing a game are discussed and does not promptly tell his club about it, will ever play professional baseball."[30] Then, upon his order, he banished the eight Black Sox players from playing in the major leagues again. The following day, most of the well-regarded newspapers supported Landis's decision, but baseball fans everywhere felt otherwise.

*   *   *   *

Fans showed an outpouring of grief for the players after Landis's decision, especially for Buck Weaver and Shoeless Joe. People sympathized with Weaver, because even though he was present at the infamous Black Sox meeting at the Ansonia Hotel, he never accepted money and played great during the series. An even greater amount of pity went towards Shoeless Joe, because he also played great during the series, he attempted to give back the five grand he received from gamblers, and mostly because everybody thought he was destined to be inducted into the Hall of Fame. Empathy for Shoeless Joe was so strong that one legend about Shoeless Joe stood the test of time. Legend has it that when he was leaving the courtroom after one of the Black Sox hearings a little boy went up to him and pleaded, "Say it ain't so, Joe. Say it ain't so." The response he gave to the boy's plea differs from story to story, but one thing that can be ascertained for sure: It was so.

Years after being kicked out of the major leagues, Shoeless Joe and Buck Weaver, in an effort to clear their names form any wrongdoing, decided to trump up charges against Comiskey in a civil suit. In the suit they claimed that somehow he tried to cover up the fix. Soon after, the case was thrown out of court. The funny thing was that neither of the two players ever approached Comiskey, or anyone else, before the eight players met at the hotel that infamous day—at which time their attempt at "coming clean" would have really made a difference.

Besides Weaver and Shoeless Joe, a number of other Black Sox players came forward to place blame on Comiskey. In their case they insinuated that they only fixed the World Series because Comiskey was not paying them enough. The fact was that it wasn't until the ashamed Black Sox players were being bombarded with questions from the press that they brought up Comiskey's stinginess. Moreover, there was no evidence to suggest that there were any arguments over contracts.[31] Basically, the ex-players were attempting to throw Comiskey under the same bus that they were driving. According to Jon Snyder in *The White Sox Journal*, "during these trials, the eight 'Black Sox' related tales of Comiskey's ill-treatment, both on the stand and to the assembled press." Snyder added, "The players' stories of Comiskey's tight-fisted practices were generally believed, leading to a change in the public perception of the White Sox owner. Were the players truthful in their portrayal of Comiskey? Or, has Comiskey been convicted by baseball historians of being a 'tightwad' based on exaggerated, false, or even perjuries testimony given by the 'Black Sox?' The historical record suggests that the latter is true."

Shadows of Chicago

There is no doubt that a few of the Black Sox players were unhappy with their salaries they were offered before the 1919 season. But, their complaints were no different than other players' from all the major league teams. Each of the owners, including Comiskey, had a business to run and each sought to have the best players for the least amount of money. So Comiskey was just doing what came normal to him—winning ball games. Conversely, the Black Sox players chose to lose ball games, thus casting the darkest shadow on professional baseball—all by themselves.

Unfortunately for Comiskey, the dark memories of the Black Sox scandal would plague him forever, and never again would he regain the wild passion he had for the game. Instead, the once fired-up owner turned into one who took a backseat to the affairs of the team. His new laid-back approach was the biggest reason his White Sox team slumped to seventh place in 1921 and would never end a season above fifth place for the remainder of his life. Amid the team's losing ways, Comiskey slowly disappeared from baseball forever. On October 26, 1931, at 72-years-old he passed away at his hunting lodge in Eagle River, Wisconsin. Rightly, he was inducted into the Baseball Hall of Fame in 1939.

*   *   *   *

The following is the final paragraph of short biography Comiskey prepared for G.W. Axelson's book, "'Commy': The Life Story of Charles A. Comiskey." The book was originally printed in 1919, and the actual biography originated before the Black Sox scandal.

The spirit of the game remains the same and that is why I take pride in being identified with it. With me baseball will never grow old. In my own estimation it may not have improved so much as many believe, but regardless of everything it is the same good old game. If I have contributed to its success I do not refer to this in the sense of boasting. I had to or fall out of the ranks. It was a fast game when I played it and the pace was hot. As fans know, I have often had trouble in keeping up with it since then, but they have been fore-bearing. What I have tried to do has been my level best.

THE END

---

[1] Shoeless Joe Jackson was once an illiterate mill-hand from South Carolina. He earned the nickname "Shoeless" after playing a game once in his socks because his shoes did not fit him. (Anderson).

[2] Snyder, John. *White Sox Journal: Year by Year & Day by Day with the Chicago White Sox Since 1901*. Cincinnati, OH: Clerisy Press.

[3] *Ibid.*

[4] Charles Comiskey, an avid patriot, donated ten percent of the gate receipts to the Red Cross, totally more than $17,000. In addition, due to labor shortage during World War I, he ordered that sheep be used to trim the lawn at Comiskey Park. (Anderson).

[5] Snyder.

[6] *Ibid.*

[7] In 1913, Charles Comiskey organized a White Sox/ Giants tour that took them to countries around the world: Japan, Hong Kong, the Philippines, Australia, India, Egypt, Italy, and England. From Liverpool, England the travel-weary players were sent home some aboard the Lusitania, the same ship sunk by a German sub on May 7, 1915, costing over 1,200 lives, including 128 Americans.

[8] Snyder.

[9] *Ibid.*

[10] The 18th Amendment was passed in 1920, prohibiting alcohol sales at ballparks until 1933.

[11] Snyder.

[12] The 1919 World Series was lengthened to nine games to make up for the loss of games during the 1918 season, due to World War I.

[13] Snyder.

[14] Anderson, Wayne. *The Chicago Black Sox Trial*. New York: Rosen Publishing, 2004.

[15] *Ibid.*

[16] Snyder.

[17] *Ibid.*

[18] *Ibid.*
[19] *Ibid.*
[20] *Ibid.*
[21] *Ibid.*
[22] Anderson.
[23] *Ibid.*
[24] Snyder.
[25] *Ibid.*
[26] *Ibid.*
[27] *Ibid.*
[28] Anderson.
[29] *Ibid.*
[30] *Ibid.*
[31] Snyder.

EPILOGUE

The Levee Denizens

Michael "Hinky-Dink" Kenna and "Bathhouse" John Coughlin

Despite their connections to the Chicago outfit and conducting their own illicit activities, Hinky-Dink and Bathhouse never saw a day in jail and never lost an aldermanic election in over forty years. Their combined political power allowed them to reign over the notorious First Ward from 1897-1938. Their control over the ward ended when Bathhouse died on November 11, 1938. He died of pneumonia at 78-years-old—along with $56,000 in horseracing gambling debts. His long-time friend, Hinky-Dink, paid for an elaborate funeral ceremony. On the other hand, when Hinky-Dink died on October, 9, 1946 at 89-years-old from diabetes, there were few people who attended his funeral. Being a scrupulous miser in his dying days, he left a substantial amount of money to his heirs—with the stipulation that $35,000 would be set aside for a mausoleum in his honor. Instead of heeding his wishes, his loving heirs bought an $85 tombstone and pocketed the rest.

Ada and Minna Everleigh

After Carter Harrison Jr. closed down the Everleigh Club in October 1911, Ada and Minna, only in their forties, skedaddled to Europe. After only six months abroad, they moved back to Chicago to try start up another whorehouse. Once they found that city no longer accepted their type of business, they took their fortunes and moved to Manhattan.

Shadows of Chicago

Upon arrival, they changed their surname to Lester. It was there that Minna lived until she died at 82-years-old in 1948. Her older sister Ada moved to Virginia, where she lived quietly until she died at 96-years-old.

Carter Harrison, Jr.

Upon closing down the Levee, and after his fifth term in office, Harrison left Chicago politics forever. After politics, he became an avid outdoorsman, traveling the U.S., Europe, and Africa. Between his many travels, he worked as a collector for the internal revenue of the northern district of Illinois until he was 84-years-old. Throughout his life he acquired many famous works of art: works by Gauguin, Cassat, and Monet were donated to the Art Institute of Chicago.33 He also found time to write two autobiographies. He died sitting at the dinner table on Christmas Day in 1953 at the age of 93.

William "Big Bill" Thompson

The last Republican mayor of Chicago, William Hale Thompson, proved to be the most flamboyant and corrupt mayors in Chicago history. Crime flourished during his administration, partly because of his close ties with outfit members like Jim Colosimo and Al Capone. Besides pledging his support for the underworld, he was also pro-German and anti-British during the World War I era—he even threatened to punch the King of England. He was also in favor of burning books in the Chicago Public Library. After Thomson died of a heart attack at the age of 74, $1,446,250 was found in his safe deposit box, much of it from his term as mayor.[1]

Johnny "The Fox" Torrio

After Colosimo's murder, Torrio ruled the Chicago outfit. His was able to run his extensive criminal network with the help of his second-in-command, Al Capone. After only four years as Chicago's vice lord, he was arrested by federal Prohibition agents. Agents acted on a tip from Torrio's biggest nemesis, Dion O'Bannion. To retaliate, Torrio had him gunned down in front of his flower shop in broad daylight. In turn, O'Bannion's gang countered by shooting Torrio in front of his home. He was taken to Jackson Park Hospital in critical condition, but would survive. Soon after, he moved back to New York and came back to Chicago only to attend court—the last time was for Capone's tax evasion trial. Like Capone, he also served a couple years for tax evasion. After that, he settled down a bit, moving with his wife to Brooklyn. He died of a heart attack in a barber's chair on April 16, 1957. He was 75-years-old. Most people weren't notified of passing until three weeks after.[2]

Al "Scarface" Capone

After people suspected him of murdering Jim Colosimo, he moved to the town of Cicero to run the Chicago outfit. After Torrio fled for New York, in only a few years, Capone built a $100 million-a-year criminal enterprise from the 1920s until 1931. During those years, his most crowning achievement was his involvement in the St. Valentine's Day Massacre, when his gang tommy-gunned seven of Bugs Moran's gang members. After he was convicted on tax evasion in 1931, he was sent to Alcatraz federal prison. He was released on parole in 1939. After his release, he began to suffer from mental and physical weakening due to syphilis. He moved to his mansion in Palm Island, Florida. He died on January 25, 1947 from cardiac arrest after suffering a stroke.

Shadows of Chicago

The Black Sox and Gamblers

Eddie Cicotte

Cicotte proved to be one of the only Black Sox players that ever admitted his guilt for fixing the World Series. After his banishment from the major leagues, he changed his name and moved to Detroit to work in the Ford plant, where he retired in 1944. After retirement, he began to talk to baseball fans. When a *Detroit Free Press* writer asked him if he suffered any guilt for fixing the Series, he answered, "I admit I did wrong, but I've paid for it. I tried to make up for it by living a clean a life as I could. Nobody can hurt me anymore." In 1969, Cicotte died in peace at the age of 84 in Detroit.[3]

Chick Gandil

Gandil, the so-called leader of the fix, was the only player to leave the White Sox before the scandal broke out. He played the 1920 season for an independent team in Idaho. There he was paid $4,000 a year, and lived off the $35,000 he (supposedly) took in from the fix. After Idaho, he played semi-pro ball in Arizona and California. Once his baseball career ended, he became a plumber in San Francisco until he retired in 1952. Defiant even in his final days, Gandil vehemently fought to clear his name of any wrongdoing. Never clearing his name, he died in 1970 at the age of 82 in Calistoga, California.[4]

Swede Risberg

Risberg, Gandil's second-in-charge, also spent the remainder of his life professing his innocence. He even attempted to sue Charles Comiskey for back pay in 1925. He received nothing in return. After his ban from the majors, he played for a semi-pro league in Sioux Falls, South Dakota. In Sioux Falls, he was booted off the team for inciting a team riot against the management. Soon after, he lost his life savings. He recovered by operating a tavern in Red Bluff, California. In 1975, he died on his 91st birthday.[5]

Happy Felsch

Like Risberg, Happy Felsch tried to sue Comiskey for back pay. In Felsch's case, he was awarded $1,166. Also claiming his innocence to the end, he raised six children in Milwaukee, worked as crane operator and a tavern owner. In 1964, he passed at 72-years-old.[6]

Lefty Williams

Williams refused to discuss the World Series fix for the rest of his life. After his ban from baseball, he pitched for several independent clubs before he moved to Chicago to operate a pool hall. After that, he moved to Laguna Beach, California to operate a plant nursery business. In 1959, he died at the age of 66.

Fred McMullin

McMullin was the least famous of the Black Sox players. Amusingly, after he was banned from baseball for taking accepting $5,000, he went into law enforcement in Los Angeles for the office of the U.S. Marshal. In 1952, he died at the age of 61.

Buck Weaver

Even though Weaver never accepted money from gamblers, Judge Landis expelled him for not turning in his fellow players involved in the fix. Weaver went on to play for a semi-pro team in Hammond, Indiana. He spent every penny of his meager paychecks on his legal appeals to get back into major leagues, but was unsuccessful. After baseball, he worked the windows at Chicago's three racetracks until his death of heart attack in 1956. He was 65-years-old.[7]

Shoeless Joe Jackson

Shoeless Joe fought harder than any other of the Black Sox players to clear his name. He even sued Charles Comiskey for $119,000 in damages for slander and breach of contract. When the trial went to court, Comiskey's attorney produced Shoeless Joe's confession that he allegedly presented to Comiskey the day after the last game of the World Series. Needless to say, the written confession destroyed his case against Comiskey. While he was in the process of litigation and afterwards, he continued to play for a number of independent teams until the age of 45. After leaving baseball forever, he ran a liquor store in Greenville, South Carolina with his wife Kate. Despite his disappearance from baseball, he frequently discussed his baseball days with the press. On one occasion, in 1951, Ed Sullivan called him for an interview on his television show to discuss his side of the Black Sox scandal. He died ten days before show was set to air. Even though his life time batting average of .356 still stands as the third highest in major league history, he was never inducted into the Hall of Fame.[8]

Arnold "The Brain" Rothstein

Rothstein was leader of the Jewish mob in New York and became known as "The Big Bankroll" among sports gamblers. He was cleared of any wrongdoing for fixing the Black Sox scandal. He was also involved with many notorious gangsters, including Charles "Lucky" Luciano. He was shot and killed over a poker game debt on November 4, 1928.

Joseph J. "Sport" Sullivan

Sullivan was never arrested and never had to testify in the Black Sox trial. Supposedly, Rothstein paid for Sulivan to flee to Mexico so he wouldn't have to appear in court to testify. After the trial, he disappeared from existence, and there is no known information about his death.

Abe "The Little Hebrew"Atell

Atell, the ex-featherweight boxing champ, was Rothstein's right hand man for decades. He was let go after the Black Sox scandal. He was never sentenced, but like Rothstein, was barred from attending any more major league baseball games. He died in New Paltz, New Jersey on Febuary 7, 1970.

The Heroes of the 1910 Stockyard Fire and Others

William J. Burroughs

Second Assistant Fire Marshal Burroughs was killed instantly at the Chicago Union Stockyards on December 22, 1910. He served 26 years and 5 months as a member of Chicago Fire Department. He was 47. He is buried at Graceland cemetery. He left behind a wife and a 12-year-old daughter.

George E. Enthof

Pipeman Enthof of Engine 23 was killed instantly at the Chicago Union Stockyards on December 22, 1910. He became a member of the fire department on October 9, 1906. He was 31. He is buried at Wunder's cemetery. His parents were in their seventies, and his brother was an engineer on Engine 99.

Shadows of Chicago

William F. Weber

Driver Walters of Engine Company 59 was killed instantly at the Chicago Union Stockyards on December 22, 1910. He became a member of the fire department on January 12, 1905. He was 34. He is buried at Mt. Olivet cemetery. He left behind a wife and three children. He almost died at the Thanksgiving Day stockyard fire about a month before the December 22 fire. He was saved some of the same men that died with him at the 1910 Stockyard Fire.

Frank W. Walters

Pipeman Walters of Engine Company 59 died after sustaining injuries at the Chicago Union Stockyards on December 22, 1910. He became a member of the fire department on October 1, 1883. He left behind a widow and two older children. He was set to retire on New Year's Day. He was the fifth member of his family to join the Chicago Fire Department. His father, retired captain, Lawrence Walter, fought at The Great Chicago Fire.

Alexander D. Lannon

Captain Lannon of Engine Company 50 died after sustaining injuries at the Chicago Union Stockyards on December 22, 1910.

Edward J. Danis

Lieutenant Danis of Engine Company 61 was killed instantly at the Chicago Union Stockyards on December 22, 1910. He is buried at Oakwoods cemetery.

Dennis M. Doyle

Captain Doyle of Engine Company 39 was killed instantly at the Chicago Union Stockyards on December 22,

1910. He is buried at Mt. Olivet cemetery next to his son Nicholas.

Nicholas Doyle

Truckman Doyle of Hook and Ladder Company 11 was killed instantly at the Chicago Union Stockyards on December 22, 1910. He became a member of the fire department on July 16, 1907. He is buried next to his father, Dennis, at Mt. Olivet cemetery. He had a wife and two children.

Nicholas Crane

Truckman Nicholas Crane of Hook and Ladder Company 18 was killed instantly at the Chicago Union Stockyards on December 22, 1910. He became a member of the fire department on January 4, 1899. He is buried at Mt. Olivet cemetery. He left behind a widow.

Charles Moore

Truckman Moore of Hook and Ladder 18 was killed instantly at the Chicago Union Stockyards on December 22, 1910. He became a member on the fire department on May 20, 1904. He is buried at Mt. Greenwood cemetery. He left behind a widow and a three-year-old daughter.

Thomas J. Costello

Pipeman Costello of Engine 29 was killed instantly at the Chicago Union Stockyards on December 22, 1910. He became a member of the fire department on August 2, 1905. He is buried at Mt. Olivet cemetery. He left behind a widow and one-year-old son.

Shadows of Chicago

William G. Strum

    Lieutenant Sturm of Engine Company 64 was killed instantly at the Chicago Union Stockyards on December 22, 1910. He became a member of the fire department on April, 14, 1897. He is buried at Mount Hope cemetery. He left behind a wife and four older daughters.

Herman Brandenburg

    Truckman Brandenburg of Hook and Ladder 11 was killed instantly at the Chicago Union Stockyards on December 22, 1910. He is buried at Oakwoods cemetery. He became a member of the fire department on March 1, 1902. He left behind a wife and two children. The day of the fire he was working on a trade with another firefighter so he could spend Christmas with his family.

James J. Fitzgerald

    Lieutenant Fitzgerald of Engine Company 23 was killed instantly at the Chicago Union Stockyards on December 22, 1910. He became a member of the department on January 1, 1905. He was to be married the following day at his home.

Michael F. McInerney

    Truckman McInerney of Truck 11 was killed instantly at the Chicago Union Stockyards on December 22, 1910. He is buried at Mt. Olivet cemetery.

George F. Murawski

    Pipeman Murawski of Engine Company 49 was killed instantly at the Chicago Union Stockyards on December 22, 1910. He is buried at Resurrection Cemetery. He had a wife and two children.

Matthew Drew

Albert J. Moriarty

Truckman Moriarty of Hook and Ladder Company 11 was killed instantly at the Chicago Union Stockyards on December 22, 1910. He became a member of the fire department on December 1, 1902. He was 34. He left behind a wife and one child. His two ballplayer brothers, William and George, both ballplayers, helped identify their brother in the ruins. They were home for a family reunion planned for Christmas Day.

Peter J. Powers

Truckman Powers of Hook and Ladder Company 11 was killed instantly at the Chicago Union Stockyards on December 22, 1910. He became a member of the fire department on December 1, 1902. He left behind a wife and two children.

Edward J. Schonsett

Truckman Powers of Hook and Ladder Company 11 was killed instantly at the Chicago Union Stockyards on December 22, 1910. He became a member on the fire department on April 1, 1907. He died on his 27th birthday and two days before his wedding anniversary.

Patrick Reaph

Reaph was a Watchman and a Special Fireman for the Nelson Morris Company for six months. He was 23-years-old when he was killed at the Chicago Union Stockyards on December 22, 1910. All of his relatives except for his sister, Bridget, lived in Ireland. He was buried at Mt. Olivet cemetery.

Shadows of Chicago

Andrew Dzurman

Dzurman was a Watchman and a Fireman for the Nelson Morris Company. He was 29-years-old when he was killed at the Chicago Union Stockyards on December 22, 1910. He is buried at Batavia cemetery. He had no relatives in Chicago.

Steven Leen

Leen was a Yard Clerk for the Chicago Junction Railroad. He was 19-years-old when he was killed at the Chicago Union Stockyards on December 22, 1910.

Widows, Orphans, and Families

It took over a year, and a long time waiting, but the victim's families were eventually compensated. The $211,000 fund was divided amongst 19 widows, 38 children, and two mothers. Most of the firefighter families carried on despite their heavy losses. Most spent the funds towards real estate and investments. Of the nineteen widows only one remarried, Alice Powers, wife of Peter Powers. Many family members never recovered after their losses.

Charles "Sy" Seyferlich

Seyferlich was born in Sweden in 1852. He entered the department in August 18, 1877. Four years after taking over the first marshal position due the deaths of Big Jim and Burroughs, Seyferlich caught a cold at a 4-11 fire that developed into pneumonia. He died at his home with his family on April 8, 1914. He was 63-years-old. He had a wife and five grown children.

Matthew Drew

Joseph Mackey

He was born on the north side of Chicago in 1880. He was the buggy driver for Big Jim Horan the day of the fire. After his injuries, he recuperated and became captain of Squad 1 in 1915. There he received numerous mentions for heroic rescues. After his promotion to battalion chief at 41 years-old, he broke the drill school record for carrying a "donut" (65 pound coil of 21/2 inch hose) up and over the top of a four-story building in 21 seconds. As second deputy fire marshal in 1934, he led his men against a fire that destroyed 90 percent of the stockyards and almost devastated the city. He retired in 1940, and moved to Wisconsin for the remainder of his life. He died in 1956 at the age of 76.

William Moore

Along with Joe Mackey, Moore was the driver for Big Jim Horan the day of the stockyard fire. After narrowly escaping death, he suffered severe injuries to his head, shoulder, hip and leg. His head injury required that he have surgery to place a silver plate in his head. After a lengthy recuperation, he was placed on disability—where he would remain for rest of his career. He moved with his family to New York City where he became an electrical engineer. After that, he worked for the federal government. He lived a long fulfilling life until his death in 1960 at the age of 73. Many years later his son Robert contacted Chicago Department historian Sully Kolomay. He presented Sully with his father's historical account of the tragedy and the bizarre dream he had the day of the fire.

Martin Lacy

In 1916, four years after surviving the 1910 fire, Chief Lacy of the 11th Battalion was responding to an alarm at the Union Stockyards. At Root and Halsted Streets, when the driver of his motor car attempted to avoid a truck, the car overturned, and he was thrown onto the street, fracturing his skull. He would die soon after at Englewood Hospital. He joined the fire department in 1885 and was present at some of Chicago's most infamous fires and is credited with numerous rescues. He died at 56-years-old. He is buried at Calvary cemetery in Evanston, Illinois. Next to his headstone, for many years, his white helmet was displayed in a glass case until it was stolen.

---

[1] Bilek, Arthur J. *The First Vice Lord: Big Jim Colosimo and the Ladies of the Levee.* Nashville: Cumberland House Publishing, 2008.
[2] *Ibid.*
[3] Snyder, John. *White Sox Journal: Year by Year & Day by Day with the Chicago White Sox Since 1901.* Cincinnati, OH: Clerisy Press.
[4] *Ibid.*
[5] *Ibid.*
[6] *Ibid.*
[7] *Ibid.*
[8] *Ibid.*

WORKS CITED

Books and Magazines

Abbott, Karen. *Sin in the Second City. Madams, Ministers, Playboys and the Battle for America's Soul*. New York: Random House, 2007.

Anderson, Wayne. *The Chicago Black Sox Trial*. New York: Rosen Publishing, 2004.

Ann Durkin Keating et al, *The Encylopedia of Chicago*, Chicago: The University of Chicago Press.

Axelson, G.W. *Commy: The Life Story of Charles A. Comiskey*. Chicago: Riley and Lee Company.

Bales, Richard F. *The Great Chicago Fire and the Myth of Mrs. O'Leary's Cow*. McFarland Press.

Chicago Fire Department Report of the Fire Marshal to City Council of the City of Chicago. January 1-December 31, 1910. p21

Connelly, Mark Thomas. *The Response to Prostitution in the Progressive Era*. Chapel Hill: North Carolina University Press, 1980.

Cronon, William. *Nature's Metropolis: Chicago and the Great West*. New York: W.W. Norton & Company, 1995.

Shadows of Chicago

D'eramo, Marco. *Pig and the Skyscrapper. Chicago: A History of our Future.* New York: New Left Books, 2002.

Flanagan, Maureen A. "Fred Busse: A Silent Mayor in Turbulent Times." *The Mayors: the Chicago Political Tradition.* Carbondale: Southern Illinois University Press, 1995.

Geoffrey Johnson, "The True Story of the Deadly Encounter at Fort Dearborn," *Chicago,* December 2009.

"The Illinois Crime Survey," *Illinois Association for Criminal Justice,* Chicago: Illinois Association for Criminal Justice, 1929.

Johnson, Curt. *Wicked City. Chicago: From Kenna to Capone.* December Press. 1994.

Bilek, Arthur J. *The First Vice Lord: Big Jim Colosimo and the Ladies of the Levee.* Nashville: Cumberland House Publishing, 2008.

Lehman-Clarkson, F.M. *White Slave Hell, or With Christ at Midnight in the Slums of Chicago.* Chicago: The Christian Witness Company, 1910.

Lindberg, Richard C. *Total White Sox. The Definitive Enclyclopedia of the Chicago White Sox.* Chicago: Triumph Books.

Mark, Norman. *Mayors Madams & Madmen.* Chicago: Chicago Review Press, 1979.

Miller, Donald L. *City of the Century. The Epic of Chicago and the Making of America.* New York: Simon and Schuster, 1996.

Paul T. Gilbert, et al. *Chicago and Its Makers: A Narrative of Events From the Day of the First White Man to the Inception of the Second World's Fair.* Chicago: F. Mendelsohn, 1929.

Rice, John. *Research Data, 1910 Stockyards Fire,* November 28, 2001.

Russo, Gus. *The Outfit: The Role of Chicago's Underworld in the Shaping of Modern America.* Bloomsbury. New York, N.Y.

Sawislak, Karen. *Smoldering City: Chicago and the Great Fire, 1871-1874.* Chicago: University of Chicago Press, 1995.

Sinclair, Upton. *The Jungle.*

Snyder, John. *White Sox Journal: Year by Year & Day by Day with the Chicago White Sox Since 1901.* Cincinnati, OH: Clerisy Press.

Tintori, Karen. *Trapped: The 1909 Cherry Mine Disaster.* New York: Atria Books, 2002.

Wade, Louise Carroll. *Chicago's Pride: The Stockyards, Packingtown, and the Environs in the Nineteenth Century.* Chicago and Urbana: University of Illinois, 1987.

Shadows of Chicago

"The Social Evil in Chicago." *Chicago Vice Commission.* 1911.

Newspaper Articles

"18-Hour Flyer Goes Into River; Fred Busse Hurt," *Chicago Daily Tribune*, February 23, 1907.

"23 Killed in Fire at Packing Plant; Chief Horan Dead," *Chicago Daily Tribune*, December 23, 1910.

"5,000 Souls and 15,000,000 a Year Tribute To Vice," *Chicago Daily Tribune*, April 6, 1911.

"Anti-Vice Plea Taken to Busse," *Chicago Daily Tribune*, Januarary 28, 1910.

"Ask Fire Reform in Stockyards," *Chicago Daily Tribune*, December 28, 1910.

"Back of the Yards," *Chicago Daily Tribune*, March 25, 1906.

"Busse Sees Levee; Changes Ordered," *Chicago Daily Tribune*, January 2, 1907.

"Big Upset in Baseball: World Series Furnishes a Complete Surprise." *Chicago Daily Tribune.* October 21, 1906.

"Burroughs Known As Hero For Rescues In Many Fires," *Chicago Daily Tribune*, December 23, 1910.

"Busse's Carreer in Politics: Product of Chicago and Known As a Man Who Does Things—Influence for Harmony" *Chicago Daily Tribune*. February 23, 1907.

"Chicago Water to Mine Fire," *Chicago Daily Tribune,* Nov 16, 1909

"Death Closes Varied Career of Fred Busse," *Chicago Daily Tribune,* July 10, 1914.

"Death of Horan to Bring Reform of Water System?," *Chicago Daily Tribune*: December 23, 1910.

"Exit Mayor Busse: Enter Mayor Harrison," *Chicago Daily Tribune,* April 18, 1911.

Fullerton, Hugh S., "'Sox'" Join 'Cubs', Pennant is Won." *Chicago Daily Tribune,* October 4, 1906.

"Heavens Forbid Pennant Raising," *Chicago Daily Tribune*. May 15, 1907.

"Horan Is Praised By Baseball Men," *Chicago Daily Tribune,* December 23, 1910.

"James Horan Address," *Chicago Daily Tribune,* August 23, 1908.

"Jim Horan Answers the Call," *Chicago Tribune*. April 14 1907.

"Jury To Seek Wire Defects As Cause," *Chicago Examiner,* December 24, 1910, Vol. 9. No. 2.

Shadows of Chicago

"Ready for High Pressure: Mayor Calls Conference On New Water System." *Chicago Daily Tribune.* May 18, 1907.

"Mayor Appoints Vice Commission: Thirty Prominent Students of Social Conditions Will Try to Solve Problem." *Chicago Daily Tribune.* March 6, 1910

"Mayor at Horan Bier," *The Daily News,* December 23, 1910.

"Message of Mayor Sends Victims Aid," *The Daily News,* December 23, 1910.

"Park Scorched: Fire Destroys 50 Cent Seats and Threatens Grand Stand," *Chicago Daily Tribune,* April 26, 1910.

"Pictures McCann As King of the Levee" *Chicago Daily Tribune.* September 10, 1909.

Sanborn, I. E., "Commy to Greet Sox Fans Today," *Chicago Daily Tribune,* July 10 1910.

Sanborn, I.E., "It Is Provided in the Rules that He Who Heels Also Shall Handle," *Chicago Daily Tribune,* Febuary 18, 1911.

Sanborn, I.E., "Sox Held For Nine Hours in Train Wreak" *Chicago Daily Tribune,* March 1, 1910.

Matthew Drew

"Sox Win World's Title, 4 To 2: Faber Beats Giants in Decisive Battle," *Chicago Daily Tribune,* October 16, 1917.

Shadows of Chicago

Matthew Drew is a veteran Chicago firefighter and also teaches firefighting tactics for the University of Illinois. He received his Masters in Writing with an emphasis on historical nonfiction from DePaul University in Chicago. He wrote for variety of publications and taught several college composition classes. He resides in Chicago with his wife and three children.

CPSIA information can be obtained at www.ICGtesting.com
Printed in the USA
LVOW12s2126010913

350333LV00004B/1/P